COVERED BY SCARS
A DIAMOND REVEALED

VISIONARY AUTHOR
RAYLONDA MCCLINTON

Foreword By Jay Morrison

© 2023 Raylonda McClinton

Book Cover Design: Dr. Shadaria Allison, Nichole Perricci, DNP Designs
Interior Book Design & Formatting: TamikaINK.com
Editor: Tee Tunnell Harris, TamikaINK.com

ALL RIGHTS RESERVED. No part of this book may be reproduced in any written, electronic, recording, or photocopying without written permission of the publisher or author. The exception would be in the case of brief quotations embodied in critical articles or reviews and pages where permission is specifically granted by the publisher or author.

LEGAL DISCLAIMER. Although the author has made every effort to ensure that the information in this book was correct at press time, the author does not assume hereby disclaim any liability to any party for loss, damage, or disruption caused by errors or missions, whether such errors or omissions result from negligence, accident, or any other cause.

Published By: Igniting The Flame Publishing

Library of Congress Cataloging-in-Publication Data has been applied for

ISBN: 9798864702642

PRINTED IN THE UNITED STATES OF AMERICA

Endorsement

Do you believe in miracles? After reading 'Covered by Scars' you will! This book will encourage your faith and help you to see that no matter what you're going through God has a future for you. Get this book and watch God not only heal you from past hurts but propel you into the amazing 'Life After' that he has for you!

>Andre Butler, Pastor,
>Faith Xperience Church

Endorsement

"Covered by Scars" is a true powerhouse of a book that lifts the veil on the incredible strength of women who've tackled their hardships head-on and emerged victorious. These 15 awe-inspiring stories are a universal reminder that healing is attainable, no matter how tough the journey may be.

Soaring with an unshakeable faith in God, this read will be a source of comfort for those in need of spiritual guidance. As you delve into the stories, you'll discover an undeniable connection to the women featured, and their experiences will help you face your own challenges with newfound hope and strength.

This book is not just a collection of stories; it's a valuable resource for anyone seeking motivation, encouragement, and insights on how to triumph over the trials that life throws our way. So, don't give up, dear reader, for your journey towards victory might be just a page away!

Saudia L. Twine, Ph.D., NCC, LPC, MFT

Table of Contents

Foreword By Jay Morrison 5

Diamond In A Rough By Raylonda McClinton 7

Shhhhh! Don't Tell Nobody By Minister Michelle Cunningham 26

The Pain and Perseverance Through Life By Tereon L. Harden............ 38

Hidden Gems By Crystal McKinley 49

Shedding The Orphan By Valila Wilson.. 59

God Is The Healer of My Scars By Angelina Rideaux............................ 75

Unbreakable By Dr. Tiffany Moore-Mellieon 85

From Tragedy To Triumph! By Zina D. Crosson..................................... 96

Blood Diamond By Marjani Chapman... 108

Beauty For Ashes By Sheray L. Laury... 118

From Victim to Victory: A Story About God's Restoring Love By Marlo McCoy 128

Dug Deep By Brandy Browning 138

No Scars Allowed By Karyn Moss 149

I Thought I Was Healed By Kenyatta Johnson.................................... 159

Clawing Out of the Muddy Pit By Niambi Carriere 175

Foreword
By Jay Morrison

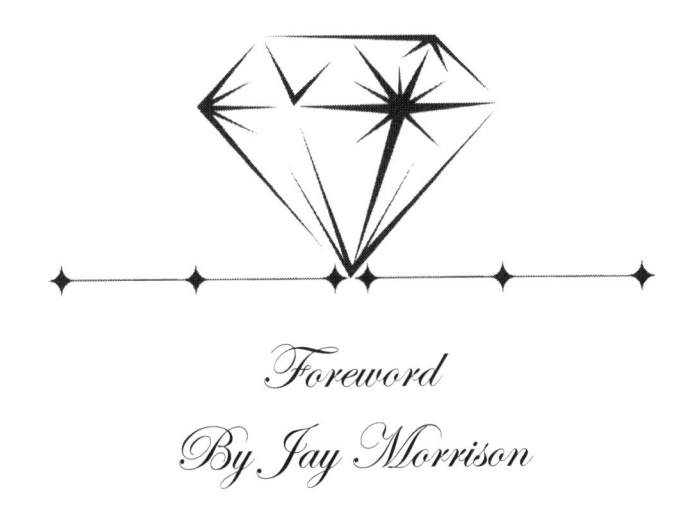

Queen Raylonda Mcclinton is a woman after God's own heart who wears her scars proudly, inspiring DIVAS around the world. I'm excited for the lives of women, families, and children that will be healed because of her obedience to bring this literary work to life. This collective of Diamonds Inspiring Virtue and Success is authoring a new testament of triumph, hope, and instructions for women around the world. I'm honored to call her a protege, a friend, and a sister for life.

JAY MORRISON

Jay Morrison
Founder, CEO & Fund Manager
Tulsa Real Estate Fund
3015 R N Martin St.
Atlanta, GA 30344
Office: 1-844-73-TULSA
Fax: 1-888-847-5915
www.TulsaRealEstateFund.com

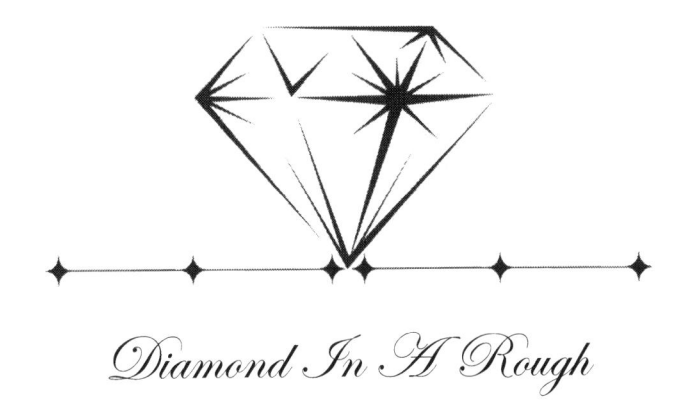

Diamond In A Rough
By Raylonda McClinton
Founder and Visionary Diamonds Inspiring Virtue
And Success

The Shaking

The door slammed, and I heard a scream saying "No! He's gone!", as I stood in the hallway leaning against the wall. I slid down the wall onto the floor, asking myself *'Who was gone? And where did they go?'* As I kept listening, I finally realized it was my hero: my grandfather, better known as Daddy. Suddenly, tears began to run down my face as I sat on the floor in a daze, not knowing what that meant for my family. My grandparents were the ones who raised me. My grandfather was the breadwinner, and grandma, Moma, was the prayer warrior.

See, I am the product of a fourteen-year-old mother and a seventeen-year-old father who knew nothing about having a baby. By the time my mother reached the young age of seventeen, she was already a married woman...but not to my father. She married another man who became my stepfather. I am so grateful for my grandparents. My grandmother played the piano for the church, and every time that blue church bus pulled up, I HAD to go. I would always think 'Why do I have to go to church with all those fake folks? All they do is gossip about each other and talk about who's sleeping with who."

That's what I would say under my breath, hoping my grandma didn't hear me. I had already decided not to attend church anymore *as soon as* I got old enough! I felt like church people were no different than the people in the world. That was my mindset growing up.

When my grandfather passed, that's when things got real. We lost our home due to unpaid taxes and had to move in with family. I went from a normal life of living in the suburbs and having the finer things in life, to being tossed to and from house to house, moving from place to place, and not having a stable place to call home. I had to keep telling myself 'Better days are coming.' My grandmother eventually moved out of state, and that's when life took a turn.

The War Within
Drugs, alcohol, and domestic abuse were heavy on both sides of my family. I watched what they did to both of my parents and my family. It was clear to me that was not how I wanted to end up. I may not have known about or understood demons and spirits at the time, but I did understand that that wasn't the road I

wanted to take, and I was determined not to end up there.

Growing up, I was Daddy's little princess. He showed me how I was supposed to be treated as a princess, but never how I was supposed to be treated as a queen. See, most men don't realize that their little princesses are watching how they treat the women in their lives. They're watching as they disrespect their mothers, they're seeing the physical, verbal, and mental abuse, all while living in the same household. They're seeing roommates–not soulmates. People who show no affection except through intimacy. There are so many women who don't know how a queen should be treated, except what has been shown to them.

Growing up, I didn't have a role model, a "shero", or a woman to look up to that I wanted to be like, so I created one, and she was me. I grew up watching the women in my life get misused, abused, and always called out their names and always had to fight. I was determined that it was not going to be me. I was determined to have my own so no one could tell me to leave. I would always hear family members whispering to one another, saying things like *"She will be like the rest of them. Watch her drop out of school, have babies, and live off welfare."* But I kept hearing these words "don't worry baby girl, you will make it" I did not understand at that time what affirmations meant, I would always speak positive over myself, even though I had no one to talk to, my grandma would always tell me to trust God and speak to Him because he hears me. I would always say, "I know she says he hears me, but I feel like he turned his back on me and not paying any attention to me." Let me ask you a question. Have you ever felt like you were pouring your heart out to God and didn't get the response you wanted, or maybe you didn't get a response at all? Well, that's exactly how I felt.

By the time I turned seventeen, I had lived with several family members, friends of the family, and neighbors. I never really got comfortable because I knew it was temporary. You're probably thinking, "She must have been bad," but that wasn't the case. Most people are comfortable with just their family and anything outside the norm they don't want to deal with. If that means helping someone, opening up your doors, clothing, or feeding someone else outside of your family or child, people don't want to go that extra mile. People boast about what they have and what they have accomplished, but ask yourself, are you using what you have been blessed with to bless others?

Matthew 25:35-37 (NKJV)
"For I was hungry, and you gave Me food; I was thirsty, and you gave Me drink; I was a stranger, and you took Me in; I was naked, and you clothed Me; I was sick and visited me; I was in prison, and you came to Me."

No Shame On Me, Shame Off Me

I know you are wondering if I graduated, and yes, I did. I quickly packed my bags and moved to Portland,

Oregon, with my mom, grandma, and family. I enrolled in Western Business College, where I took up legal secretary/administration. I knew Portland was not the place for me. I tried to find a job, but no one would hire me, so I began hustling and selling drugs. I graduated a year later and came back to Detroit, Michigan. I started working for law firms and finally got hired at the courts.

By age 24, I was pregnant with my son. Of course, everyone wants to have their child with someone they love and marry, but that wasn't my case. My son's father was a legally married but separated man. I didn't want a child nor a relationship with him, but that lust spirit will take you down a slippery slope that you don't have brakes for. When I found out I was pregnant, I quickly decided I wasn't keeping the baby. I discussed this with my doctor, who reminded me that I had always had problems with my fallopian tube, and that most women like myself never get pregnant or have an ectopic pregnancy. My doctor looked me in the face and said, "All I'm going to say is that you have never tried to carry a baby before, and you don't know if this one will make it, but it is in the right place." Once he told me that, I asked myself, "Are you mentally, physically, emotionally, and financially ready for this?" I wanted a baby one day, but I wasn't sure if I was ready now. I quickly changed my mind and began to see a future with my baby. What I called a mistake, God performed a miracle; where I saw pain, God saw purpose.

Pain To Purpose

April 1, 1998, was the best day of my life; the day my young king was born. I never could've imagined how he would change my life. Two years later, I bought a house. In 2004, I injured myself on the job, resulting in me losing my job, my home, and my car. Worst of all, my son and I had to stay with someone again. I instantly blamed God, crying and yelling "God, how could this happen to me again? I serve you, I'm doing what you told me to do, I'm not living in sin, and I am walking with you! How could you allow me and my baby to be without!?" I immediately heard God tell me "But daughter, you are not without. See, I promised you I would never leave you nor forsake you. You have shelter, you have food, and you are in a safe place. I have not rejected you; I am right here. Even through the storm, you are safe in my arms. I am your Jehovah Jireh, your provider."

Hebrews 13:5 (KJV)
"Let your conversation be without covetousness, and be content with such things as ye have: for he hath said, I will never leave thee, nor forsake thee."

Philippians 4:19 (KJV)
"But my God shall supply all your needs according to his riches in glory by Christ Jesus."

From the moment my son came into the world, I promised myself I wouldn't take him through what I went through. So I was determined to get back on my feet and get there quickly. I began styling hair at a salon and quickly gained clientele. One morning, as you know, I got that special knock on the bedroom door, saying me and my son had to find somewhere else to stay. I knew it was time to start a spiritual fast, so I could hear my directions from God clearly. I promptly began to apply for apartments, praying that my 2004 foreclosure wasn't on my credit report. Even though I had no money saved, I kept doing what God told me to do. He told me to write the vision and make it plain.

Habakkuk 2:2-3 (KJV)

"And the LORD answered me, and said, Write the vision, and make it plain upon the tables, that he may run that readeth it. For the vision is yet for an appointed time, but at the end, it shall speak, and not lie; though it tarry, wait for it; because it will surely come, it will not tarry."

I began to declare the details of my vision. Where I wanted to live, what I saw in my home, and how many rooms and bathrooms. Finally, one of my applications for an apartment got approved! My son and I were on our own again. My mom also came to live with me and my son. She had already stopped doing drugs, but that alcohol and nicotine demon was still there. I watched her begin to come to church, and I began to see the deliverance taking place. She has now been free from drugs, alcohol, and cigarettes for years. I'm so proud of her! I watched her retire from her job after fifteen years, credit, cars, and God. Don't tell me what God can't do!! Even though she wasn't there for me growing up, she gets a trophy for being the best grandmother, and I am truly thankful for our mother and daughter relationship today.

I always talked about leaving the church, but the church was always in me. So, even when I wasn't attending church, everyone would always say I sounded like a minister. In 2006 I was ordained as an evangelist, and quickly threw my license up in my bedroom closet. See, I have a thing about titles. I saw people with positions in high places abuse their titles all my life. I would always say jokingly (yet, seriously) "I don't care what you call me, just don't call me late for dinner." Many people don't know how to handle authority. They abuse and misuse it. Today I am now ordained as an evangelist and as a minister, yet I always say "God, keep me humble, and whatever you need me to do for the house of the Lord or your people, I will do."

Crushed Diamonds Still Shine
In 2010, I opened my salon called A Touch Of Heaven Salon. In 2012, I promised my grandma I would get her the house of her dreams. The day before we moved into the house I promised her, she died. She never saw the house. Talk about being crushed! It took a lot out of me to keep pushing through. See, I was always called my grandma little Mini Me (Little Ginnie). Once I moved and settled in the new house, I started a women's

group called The Diamonds Ministry, and hosted the group at my house. In 2013, I came across a guy named Mr. Jay Morrison. He had written a book called Hip Hop to Homeowners. One of my partners asked me to order his book for them, but it was only an ebook. So, I downloaded it to my phone and began reading it. I began researching him and discovered he was opening Jay Morrison Academy in January 2014. Long story short, I took his twelve-month course, closed my first deal in six months, and bought and flipped two properties in nine months. Since then, I have done over 90 deals part-time. I am so grateful because it changed me and my son's lives.

By walking in my purpose through hair styling and selling homes, I was able to send my son to college, I was able to pay for my son's apartment, and get him THROUGH college. My son graduated from Los Angeles Film School in 2020 with a bachelor's in Filming and Directing. I ran my business for seven years, the year of completion. At that point, I closed my salon and started a new beginning.

Change Agents

In 2016 God woke me up and told me to seal the name "DIVAS". I was like "...that's not GOD; that's the devil! DIVAS is **not** in the Bible." God began to show me that it was an acronym.

Even though it was an acronym, God told me to take the periods out. When the church sees DIVAS, they cringe; but when the world sees it, they get excited.

God said, "Daughter, I am sending you back for the lost at all costs." Then, I was commissioned to do a conference. I didn't know what that meant, or where to even begin. I immediately called my cousin Tiffany and told her what God said. I just knew she would think I was crazy, because it sounded crazy to me, lol, but she believed me even when I was second-guessing myself. God will send you someone who will see the vision that God gave you and will help you run with it. And so it was.

DIVAS - Diamonds Inspiring Virtue And Success: Women from all walks of life united to strengthen, encourage, equip, and educate entrepreneurship, virtue, and success into the women of God.

I immediately started laughing, saying "God, it's only me." Who would have known that through my obedience, at the end of my conference women would stand up one after another and testify? One woman said she would have killed herself if she had not attended. Another woman got up and testified how she was so thankful for being there, because she had just looked over at a Mack truck while she was driving and said to herself "If I drove my car up under this truck, there wouldn't be anyone who would miss me." Another woman stood up and said "I am so thankful for coming here, because I'm pregnant again, and I was thinking of committing suicide and I was going to take my babies with me." I couldn't do anything but cry because I was in my feelings and didn't think God could use me.

See, DIVAS was birthed through my pain. I, myself, was hurt, and didn't think God could use me in that state. God told me "Not only am I going to use you, Daughter, but what you thought was a mess was all part of your message, and what you thought was pain was all part of your purpose. Your life is going to help change others." I was so confused, but now I see. As I write this, we are preparing for our fifteenth empowerment women's conference, scheduled for November 2023. Women worldwide have joined together for break-out sessions and leave with breakthroughs. They come in empty and leave out birthing "babies" all over the world. These aren't natural babies, but spiritual ones. Visions and promises that God placed inside of them to cultivate, nurture, and bring to life. Businesses, books, speakers, and entrepreneurs have come forth out of these conferences. Women are rising, turning around, and helping other sisters rise. DIVAS has put a stamp in Detroit, Michigan, and set a blaze worldwide. DIVAS is known for our Bridge The Gap community outreach events, where we join forces with other businesses to help serve communities.

In 2020, God shifted us when the world shut down for COVID. We didn't stop. While everyone else was scared to come in contact with people, DIVAS was still out in the streets serving, clothing, feeding, and loving on God's people without shelter. In 2021, I was introduced to an app called Clubhouse. Who would have known that DIVAS would shift from a private conference call five days a week to an app where people could connect with us freely from anywhere in the world? God had me start a room–I'm so thankful for my DIVAS sister Keyona, who agreed to join me. So many women have been blessed by the WAKE, PRAY, SLAY, COMMAND YOUR DAY room. God created a safe space where women could release their hurt and be refilled by love and the word of God. Where they could release the pain and push towards their promise. I have watched women who were abused, misused, former drug addicts and alcoholics, molested, raped, and so much more, get healed and set free just by coming to our events, coming on my Facebook live videos or participating in Clubhouse. See, the devil wants you to hold onto things that have happened in the past, but God wants you to release those things and forgive them.

Philippians 3:13-14(KJV)
"Brethren, I count not myself to have apprehended, but this one thing I do, forgetting those things which are behind, and reach forth unto those things which are before, I press toward the mark of the prize of the high calling of God in Christ Jesus".

Covered By Scars, A Diamond Revealed

Through the clubhouse app and our DIVAS events, women worldwide have truly been healed and set free. We have so many testimonies that I can't tell them all, but God created this book so that these fifteen women authors could share their stories and God's true Glory.

God birthed this Anthology out of me and called it "Covered By Scars, A Diamond Revealed". I never saw a book inside of me, nor saw myself as the visionary of a book with fifteen authors impacted by this one organization called DIVAS. But this book details many testimonies of how when women come together on one accord, they are a FORCE TO BE RECKONED WITH. This book was created to show women that no matter what has happened in their past, there is still a diamond underneath all those scars. I truly understand that it was not me but the God in me. See, DIVAS understands that God uses women to help other women, but our main focus is pointing them to God's word. God is looking for vessels he can use. ANYONE can be used, no matter what your past is, what anyone says about you, or how many obstacles come your way. You are not a Victim, but a Victor. Always remember, ***it doesn't dim your light to shine light on another diamond. It only makes your light shine brighter when you put your lights together.***

Proverbs 31:10
Who can find a virtuous woman? For her price is far above rubies.

FIVE KEY POINTS TO REMEMBER:

- Seek God
- Spend Time with God
- Trust God

- Know God
- Rest in God

People always ask me "Why are you always smiling and why do you always go out of your way to help others?" I just smile and say to myself "If only you knew what I've been through, you would turn around and help someone else too."
I am so grateful to God because I was that DIAMOND IN THE ROUGH.

Dedication

SON-SHINE

I am dedicating this chapter to my son, Jamir McClinton. Thank you for being my Son-Shine. You are truly my WHY. You help me to be the best version of me. You have always been there when no one was there. You have seen your mother in her worst days and always encouraged me. You would grab my face and kiss me even when you couldn't talk. God broke the mode when he created you, and I will forever be grateful that he chose me to be your mother. I love you son. What moma always says is ONLY UP FROM HERE.

MY ANGEL

I also would like to dedicate this chapter to my grandmother. Thank you, Mom, for instilling the best gift anyone could ever give to someone, and that was God. Thank you for leading me to Christ. Thank you for showing me how to trust God even when I couldn't trace him. I am forever grateful to you, Mom. Rest up; seeing each other again will never be a goodbye. You are my special angel.

ACKNOWLEDGEMENT

First, I want to acknowledge God for inspiring me to birth this book and giving me the strength to endure the obstacles that come my way. I want to thank

God for Dr. Allen for seeing the vision that God gave me and accepting the challenge to take this project on with the DIVAS; I would like to thank my Pastor Andre Butler for seeing the vision that God has put in me and for endorsing my book.

Thank you to my brother from another mother, Mr. Jay Morrison, who has been my A1 from Day 1. Thank you, brother, for instilling in and seeing the gift in me when I didn't see it in myself. For always pushing me to run with the vision and go after what God showed me. I am truly thankful for God using you to help many people generate wealth worldwide. Keep allowing God to use you. Thank you, Dr. Tiffany Mellieon, for not only being my rider, sister, and cousin who has truly stuck closer than a friend. I can't begin to write about us because it would truly be a part 2 and 3, but you already know I thank you and appreciate you. I love you for all you do in front and behind the scenes. You have truly been there.

Thanks, sis; I would like to thank Dr. Saudia Twian for always being there for the DIVAS. You have been a blessing to us for so many years, and words can't describe how you have helped so many sisters get free. Thank you for your obedience. I love you all.

This book is dedicated to ALL THE WOMEN that will read and study this book. These are ALL real-life stories, but we want you to know that GOD GETS ALL THE GLORY. I pray you are just as blessed as we were when God told us to release it. I pray for healing, deliverance, and breakthroughs through these chapters. I pray that God's anointing flows and saturates the rooms as the people of God read these chapters. God, you are so good, and I can't thank you enough for all that you have done and keep on doing.

Raylonda McClinton

Raylonda McClinton is an Ordained Minister, International Transformational Life Coach, Real Estate Developer, and the Founder and CEO of Shining Diamond Real Estate LLC, WOW Women Of Wealth LLC, and DIVAS (Diamonds Inspiring Virtue And Success), a 501(c)(3) nonprofit organization. Her mission is to educate, equip, empower, and encourage women through entrepreneurship, virtue, and success. Raylonda is passionate about helping others, and through her passion, she has positively influenced countless lives through various community outreach efforts, inspirational speaking, empowerment sessions, and mentoring. Raylonda was born and raised in Detroit, Michigan, and is a single mother of one son! She is dedicated to finding solutions that will impact the City of Detroit and surrounding areas as well as transforming the lives of everyone she encounters.

Raylonda McClinton
Shining Diamond Realestate
(248)595-2372

Shhhhh! Don't Tell Nobody
By Minister Michelle Cunningham

For years, trying to fit in and feel accepted and wanted was a struggle. I had gone through life in a whirlwind of ups, downs, twists, and turns, from having two beautiful daughters by the time I was sixteen years old, to the trauma of being molested from the age of seven to eight, abandoned by my mother who gave me to my grandmother at a very young age and raped at the age of twenty. I felt used, abused, and alone, and I thought, with all I had been through, who would want me? Why is all of this happening to me, and if there is a God, where is He?

Sometimes, we feel like God has left us, doesn't care about what we are going through, or is just ignoring us, but I am a living witness to the fact that is not true. I learned that God promised me in His Word in Deuteronomy 31:8(KJV), which says, "And the LORD, he it is that doth go before thee; he will be with thee, he will not fail thee, neither forsake thee: fear not, neither be dismayed.

It is a book of inspirational poems God gave me, believe it or not, all in my sleep except for one that tells my story. Even though we don't always understand everything we go through one thing for sure: God loves us, and we are the Apple of His Eyes. God is the creator of all things; there is nothing He does not know, so be strong and courageous because He is in your corner and will not fail or forsake you. We serve an awesome God!

As I tried to weather the storms of life with two children and learn how to maneuver through this world, I found myself looking for love in all the wrong places, not even knowing what love was. All my life, I was told things like, "You ain't going to be nothing; you need to go home and raise them, babies; you are used up now. Nobody wants a girl with no education and two babies already, and then, to top it all off, they would tell me if someone did want to be bothered with me, it's only for what's between my legs and not my ears." I would respond to them by telling my nanna what they were saying to me, and they said, SHHH! Don't Tell Nobody. They won't believe you anyway, and this was not the first time I had heard those words. It was the words the man who molested me would say as I was crying; he would tell me SHHH!!! Don't tell anybody; I will hurt your grandmother and mom if you do. I believed him, and to this day, my mother and grandmother have gone on to glory and never knew what he did to me.

For years, I walked around holding this secret in

me along with the guilt, the shame, and the embarrassment, always thinking that all of this was my fault and later learning that none was my fault. It was the fault of the abuser in his sickness. So, I realized that healing begins with recognizing the abuse and the damage that it has done.

As the healing continues in your life, as you learn to walk with Jesus, trust in Jesus, and give Him your pain, you begin to feel free. Someone once told me that we have to be willing to be covered by God after being covered with so many scars of life, and we have to be open to revealing everything to God so He can heal. We must learn to tell ourselves, "Yes, we've been through some things, but we're still here," and when the enemy tries to tell us to SHHH, keep everything to ourselves and don't tell nobody. We have to know the power we have because the enemy is telling us to be silent, but in reality, we have to speak it for healing. God says to release it, surrender all, and turn it over to Jesus; he will make it alright. In the words of the late theologian E. Stanley Jones, "Surrender the thing you fear into the hands of God. Turn it to God and ask Him to solve it with you. Fear is keeping things in your own hands; faith is turning them over into the hands of God and leaving them there." I can now honestly say that scars once covered me, but now I am a diamond worth more than gold.

You know that old saying, "looking for love in all the wrong places," that was me. It was me who saw what I wanted, stepped into it, and took it from there, not knowing what I was looking for; in my mind, it was just "something to do," I guess you can say I was truly looking for love in all the wrong places and trying to get it from people who didn't even have a clue. But I finally realized that what I was looking for was not real love because I didn't know exactly what love was. I knew what it looked like on TV, and I knew what it looked like in magazines, but I never had a real example of what true love was or what it was to be a part of something that showed love. What is love, and where can I find someone to love me?

That was the question I always asked myself. Unbeknownst to myself, I started reading God's Word, not comprehending and understanding what the Word was saying, but I knew that to learn who I was and whose I was, I had to become intentional in my search for His Word. I read one day a scripture that answered my question about love. 1 John 4:16 (KJV) says, "And we have known and believed the love that God hath to us. God is love; and he that dwelleth in love dwelleth in God, and God in him." and in Jeremiah 31:3 (KJV) says, " The LORD hath appeared of old unto me, saying, Yea, I have loved thee with an everlasting love: therefore with lovingkindness have I drawn thee" When I read these scriptures I realized that not only is God love but His love for me is everlasting meaning that He had loved me from the beginning of time before He even placed me in my mother's womb. He continues to love me every day, faults and all.

I remember there was a song I used to sing when I was young and didn't realize what it was telling me; it says, "Jesus loves me. This I know for the Bible tells me so." How do I know that Jesus loves me? He died for me on an old rugged cross, and God showed how much He loves me while I was out there looking for love in all the wrong places, laying and playing in places I should not have been in, and for all that, the Word says, "while we were still sinners, He sent His Son Jesus Christ to die for us." I now know what love is, and it's the best thing I have ever known. God Is Love, and He loves me for eternity; he loves my past, present, and future. With all certainty, I now know that I have that Agape love that only God can give me, so I will no longer be quiet, and I will no longer listen when I am told to SHHH...... I have learned that stillness is no longer my portion. I will run expeditiously and tell everybody about the love of my Heavenly Father.

Now, I still sometimes go through life's issues, circumstances, and problems day by day, feeling like there is no hope, I have no dreams, no goals, and nothing to look forward to. It made me feel like I was very boring, so I thought. I thought I was okay; after all, I had five beautiful children and was still not married, but I was thinking maybe one day, I would have a job, a house, and a car; what else could I possibly need? I thought to myself. I learned that I am not my situation, that God is with me, that God has me, that God surrounds me every day, that my life is tailor-made just for me, and that there is no one else like me. But there are those days that I think, why me, God? I know what Your Word says about me, but I feel that I am just someone who doesn't understand sometimes my significance to you.

In this healing process, I am learning that when I pray or converse with God, He will answer me or bring something back to my remembrance, perhaps a scripture, a song, a movie, or even a person to confirm what He has said or told me to do. In Ephesians 2:10 it says, "For we are his workmanship, created in Christ Jesus unto good works, which God hath before ordained that we should walk in them." I realized that Jesus Christ created me for a divine purpose and made me, as some might say, "the Bomb-dot-com," despite my flaws and shortcomings. I have learned that I am not alone in this life journey and that we all are going through something. Even as a woman of God, I still go through doubts, fear, and unbelief, and guess what? It's okay.

I read a book called "It is Okay Not to Be Okay, Moving Forward One Day at a Time." This book has helped me learn how to deal with those feelings by knowing it's okay and that I was created to go through them. Listen, there have been days that I felt like all hope was gone. I wanted to throw in the towel and stay in bed with my head under the covers, but God sent my DIVAS sisters, who told me not on their watch, that I was to get up and know that God had me no matter what. They told me that He said in His Word that He will never leave or forsake me, no matter what. I thank God because He has brought me a long way from alcoholism, sex addictions, people pleasing, low self-esteem, guilt, shame, and broken heartedness, and some of these I am still a work in progress. Still, in all actuality, He sent His Son Jesus to die for me so that I could live and have life and have it more abundantly. We serve a sovereign and merciful God who loves us. If you don't know of this love, I offer you Jesus Christ, my Lord and Savior, and if He did it for me, He will do it for you; no matter what you have done in your life, all you have to do is read Romans 10: 9-10, 13 confess with your mouth, believe in your heart and live according to His will.

Now, I must say that after being told about the Bible and learning to read scriptures like Psalm 17:8, which states that I am the Apple of God's eyes and Psalm 139:13-14 where God says that I am fearfully and wonderfully made, I started to think about myself, I began to learn who God says I am. However, I was still scared to tell anybody I feared what people would think about me. Well, this was something I had never done before. So, what changed? What brought me out of the place of blackness, gloom, and obscurity? Well, I am glad you asked. I was blessed to meet a group of women, a sisterhood called the DIVAS on this Clubhouse app, in a room called Wake Pray, Slay, and Command Your Day.

I came across this room one day, looking for another room with a similar name. In this room, these women were talking, praying, and sharing their stories, and this woman had the most powerful, eloquent, compelling voice I had ever heard and after coming into the room several times around 6:45 a.m. Monday through Friday, I had an aha moment. This was what I had been looking for; I was so captivated by the power and the energy. I remember she told the sisters there was no competition, only camaraderie in this sisterhood because, let the world tell it, women can't get along.

One day, I came in, and she invited me to join them. I felt like I was nobody; I didn't have the poise and eloquence of these ladies, and I certainly didn't know scripture like them. So I asked myself why she asked me to join them. I didn't know these ladies from a can of paint. Oh But God!! This was in 2021, and I am still blessed by the wisdom and knowledge my sisters share daily.

One of my DIVAS sisters told me, "No shame on you, Shame off you," I had to know who I was to help someone else and that it was not my situation, that God was with me, that God has me and that He surrounds me every day, so I should wake up and know that it is a new day to start in a new way. Through the help of my sisters, I learned that I was no longer a captive. Romans 8:15 (KJV) says, "For ye have not received the spirit of bondage again to fear; but ye have received the Spirit of adoption, whereby we cry, Abba, Father" I no longer have to fear the old life that I once had because of Jesus Christ, I have a new life now that is living by the Spirit. I learned that we are children of the Most High, and when we truly understand our freedom, we can then begin to let go of those areas in our lives that held us captive, held us back, and held us down. We can learn to LET GO AND LET GOD! NO MORE SHHH!!!

Acknowledgments

    I would like to acknowledge my beautiful daughter Michele La'Rae Blainefield-Edwards who went home to be with the Lord in June 2022; she is truly missed and will never be forgotten.. To my children, grandchildren, and family, I would like to say that I appreciate and love you all for your support in all my endeavors. To my DIVA sisterhood, I say thank you so much for being the hands that pulled me up when I was down and being my strength when I was weak. I appreciate you all for being on this journey with me, and I look forward to seeing what God has planned for our family. I love you all, and thank God for allowing me to be your mom, your friend, your sister and family member.

GOD BLESS YOU!!!
Love,
Minister Michelle Cunningham

Minister Michelle Cunningham

The journey between what you once were and who you are now becoming is where the dance of life really takes place, a quote by Barbara De Angelis. To dance with the Father, life will never be the same. You take my hand in a swirl and a spin, Asking my daughter, "Where have you been?" You close your eyes and call My name, Yet you dance with hurt, sorrow, and shame... a poem written by Michelle Cunningham.

    Michelle Cunningham is a successful author, entrepreneur, CEO, and founder of The Lucy's House of Daughters, a home for first-time young mothers, and Princess Moos Child Care Center, which is a safe and affordable place for our young mothers to leave their babies. She has an Associate in Specialized Business majoring in Medical Business Administration, Associate in Medical Secretary, and she is presently working for the Allegheny Health Network in Pittsburgh, PA. She is a National Certified Insurance & Coding Specialist since 2004.

    Her passion is for young mothers, especially since she was a young mother of two at the age of 16. She has a servant's heart, always ready to lead and assist. She was licensed to preach the gospel on Nov 21, 2014, at Emmanuel Baptist Church in Rankin, PA, and now, as an Associate Minister of Triedstone Baptist Church, she serves the people of God as a Sunday School Teacher, Women's Ministry Facilitator for the Single and Satisfied Ministry and Spiritual Leader of the Selfless Intercessory Prayer Warriors Ministry. She is a member of the Pastor's Guild and the Missionary Ministry. Believing in the power of prayer, she has hosted a Prayer Line each morning utilizing the Marco Polo app beginning at 6:30 a.m. for the last four years. In 2017, God told her to start the Women of Distinction Ministry, which she started in her home, and that year, she was able to bless a women's shelter with care packages and gifts.

Michelle is the proud mother of 5 children: Siddeequah, Nicole, Isaac (Rae), Michele (Kyle), and Mikey(Brea), and a grandmother of nine.

Contact Minister Michelle Cunningham
Email: MichelleCunningham06012022@gmail.com
wodm2023@gmail.com
lucyhouse50213@gmail.com
Instagram: mickeymichelle61
Facebook: Michelle Cunningham
Min Michelle Cunningham

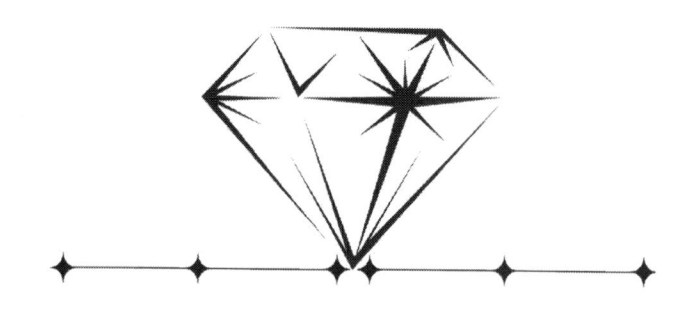

The Pain and Perseverance Through Life
By Tereon L. Harden

Often, Life circumstances and challenges can take the life out of you. We all want successful careers. We all want to say we made it. One moment, your life will feel like everything is okay. The next moment, a circumstance challenge will turn your life upside down. A bad experience or drastic change will make you scared. You feel like you are on an island alone.

In 2011, I was hit with a serious medical diagnosis at the height of my successful career and a few months away from receiving a Master's in Human Services. My life took a downward spiral. I remember thinking, "This can't be happening now." I stared at the physician in complete shock and responded, "Not me, I'm healthy with no underlying conditions." The physician said, "We need to admit you for further testing and confirm the diagnosis."

The news had me feeling hopeless, as if I was on a bed of thorns, and as if this was my ending. Because of the seriousness of the diagnosis, I was put in isolation. No visitor contact was allowed except by phone or fully gowned. This unexpected event discouraged me. I did not know what to do next. Still in disbelief, I had to be strong to take the test and get the results. I decided I did not want visitors other than my mother, who was alive then. I explained everything to her. I had to suck it up and prepare for the next few days and weeks. To prepare myself, I had to persevere through the doubt and pain. I had to rely on prayer. I had to pray fervently. Despite what it looked like then, I had to have faith in God. Finally, I had to have an attitude to help me live daily, come what may.

Perseverance Through Doubt and Pain

"But when you ask, you must believe and not doubt because the one who doubts is like a wave of the sea, blown and tossed by the wind. That person should not expect to receive anything from the Lord. Such a person is double-minded and unstable in all they do (James 1:6-8, NKJV)."

Challenges and setbacks will cause us to have doubt and, in most cases, reveal what we're made of when problems knock at our door. The book of James talks about "the one who doubts is like a wave of the sea (James 1 6-8)." I had multiple tests to take the next morning and had to wait over four days for results. I wasn't allowed any food. I was on a liquid diet. I could feel doubt creeping in and felt I would never get better. My mother, who was alive then. I remember her saying, "Pray". Try to get some rest. I'll be there in the morning." At that moment, I felt all I had was God. I needed a miracle right away. So, I took the chance to bask in his presence. I said, "Lord, this pain is real." Then, I asked God to remove any doubt and pain.

Relying On Prayer

"God grant me the serenity to accept the things I cannot change, courage to change the things I can, and wisdom to know the difference. Living one day at a time; enjoying one moment at a time; accepting hardships as the pathway to peace; taking, as He did, this sinful world as it is, not as I would have it; trusting that He will make all things right if I surrender to His Will; so that I may be reasonably happy in this life and supremely happy with Him forever and ever in the next." Amen.

Sometimes, situations in life will lead you to increase your prayer life. I lived in a single-parent home with my mother and on the weekends with my great-grandmother. As a child, I remember hearing my mother and great-grandmother praying all day and night. Among the prayers they said were the Lord's Prayer and the Serenity Prayer. I never thought two simple prayers could help me navigate a difficult diagnosis and the challenge I now face as an adult.

Sadly, it took a whirlwind to shake my world and lead to a deeper and more consistent prayer life. That life lesson has taught me to pray daily. Although my mother prayed for me, I had to pray for myself to get through what looked like the end. During the most challenging nights and days of my life, prayer was all I had to communicate to heal my body.

Fervent Prayer

"Confess your trespasses to one another, and pray that you may be healed. The effective, fervent prayer of a righteous man avails much. (James 5:16, NKJV)"

Although it was a difficult season in my life, I wanted the Lord to know I was sincere in my prayers for healing. On some days, I still felt my prayers were not answered. I felt there was more required of me. I would pray and still feel somewhat hopeless. One day, I fell, with the words, "The prayers of the righteous avail," ringing in my mind, and I began to cry out fervently to the Lord. I believed it was the only way to pray for healing.

"And will not God surely see to it that justice is done to his chosen ones who cry out to him day and night, and will he delay toward them? I tell you that he will see to it that justice is done for them soon (Luke 18:7-8(d), NKJV)!" As I prayed fervently day and night, I felt warmth all over my body. I understood the difference. I was calling out, asking for forgiveness. I am asking for the Lord's will to take place, and I thank God for choosing me to handle this task. I cried out, "Come what may in my life." I was more consistent in my prayer life and felt my prayers were answered as I began to pray fervently to the Lord.

Relying On Faith

"So, Jesus said to them, "Because of your unbelief; for assuredly, I say to you, if you have faith as a mustard seed, though refined by fire—may result in praise, glory, and honor when Jesus Christ is revealed. 1 Peter 1:6-7, NIV

When the physician diagnosed me with the spirit of lung disease, I had to have faith and exercise my faith to get through. It was easy to accept the diagnosis. Despite my fear and being on the verge of full-blown panic, I continued to press on, have faith, and wait for the test results. My precious mother said, "Have faith in a mustard seed."

Faith in God was the most valuable thing I learned during my illness. It would be best if you believed you could overcome. You have to embrace your adversity to deal with it. I don't mean to be content. Hold on to scriptures like "I can do all things through him who strengthens me (Philippians 4:11-13). I drew a board to encourage myself. I had to have the faith of a mustard seed that things would work out regardless of its appearance. Life is challenging, but your faith has to remain steadfast.

Living Daily with Our Challenges

Daily, I tried to gain perspective on my situation and how I would adjust my life to live with what the physician said was the spirit of lung disease. It was hard to grasp and make adjustments. I had to change my eating habits completely. I went from eating whatever to eating healthy. The disease had no known cure back then. The only medication to manage the pain and swelling is a steroid. I still remember the day I researched this steroid to learn more about it. I recall the knot that formed in my stomach after googling and realizing the side effects of the steroid that I had to endure.

Feeling unprepared, I scheduled bi-weekly meetings with the medical staff. I put together a support system of family and friends. I was on a reduced work schedule, regardless of the pressure from my job. My mom took care of me like I was a kid. I decided not to allow the spirit of lung disease to take over my life but to live my life to the fullest.

"So that your faith might not rest on human wisdom but God's power (1 Corinthians 2:5, NKJV)."

I relied on God to lead me. I decided to control what I could control. All other issues out of my control were left at my house or the church altar. I decided to travel and go to concerts, football games, and basketball games. My thought was to embrace and have fun regardless of my circumstances. I'm living out some of the best days of my life since my diagnosis. I've earned several race medals. I have been to other countries like Italy, Australia, Hong Kong, China, and Japan, to name a few; I also make plans to visit Hawaii yearly. "For whatever is born of God overcomes the world. And this is the victory that has overcome the world—our faith. (1 John 5:4, NJKV)"

Although we go through life and deal with setbacks, challenges, and circumstances, the beauty is the pain is temporary. The initial pain of the diagnosis did sting. It hurts. On many days, the illness takes the life out of me. I can't control what is happening all the time. However, I have total control over how I respond to this to the spirit that struck me at the height of my career and success. I decided not to feel sorry for myself but instead respond positively to the press and get through.

"And the Holy Spirit helps us in our weakness. For example, we don't know what God wants us to pray for. But the Holy Spirit prays for us with groanings that cannot be expressed in words (Romans 8:26, NLT)."

Instead of folding, I developed a better prayer life. Prayer is my daily substance. I connected with The Divas prayer group, where I Pray daily with this beautiful group of ladies. I'm held accountable by them. My faith in God is unmovable. I understand pain is temporary and must persevere through what looks bad. Even though I was diagnosed with the spirit of lung disease, I refuse to be defeated despite the many challenges.

"I have set the Lord always before me; because He is at my right hand, I shall not be moved. Therefore, my heart is glad, and my glory rejoices; my flesh will rest in hope (Psalm 16:8-9, NKJV)."

The physician claims it's no cure for the lung disease. I have experienced pain that comes and goes, but I know that God is the healer of my faith, and I've decided to fight the good fight of faith, and I know better days are ahead.

This ordeal has made me a better person and allowed me to focus on the value of life. I did receive my Master's degree the same year I was diagnosed. I'm currently a successful business owner. I'm determined to get the word out about this disease that lives dormant and will feaster out of nowhere. If I could leave you with any encouragement after this setback, I would recommend praying and staying faithful to God. Keep the faith and continue to Persevere Through the Pressure and Pain in life. Life will deal all of us blows, but we must embrace and know God will never leave or forsake us.

Acknowledgments

This chapter is dedicated to my late Mother, Lillie B. Harden. I look at my phone daily to hear your voice. I'm a better person because of you. Your unconditional love is unmatched. If I can do anything like you, I want to live and love others as I saw you do. I laughed at you for giving your last away. Now, I model you for faithfulness to God, family, friends, and other family members who called you "mom." I love you, Mommy. Rest Well! Tee, your middle child.

Tereon L. Harden

Business Owner and Author Tereon L. Harden enjoys giving back to the community. She lives in Atlanta, Georgia, with her immediate family.

She earned a Masters in human resources in 2012. She worked in the Healthcare field for the same organization for over 20 years. She realized her true passion and launched Tereon Tee Harden LLC in 2017, where she worked to bring dreams to reality for homeowners. She was diagnosed in 2012 with a terminal lung disease. She lost her Mother and best friend in 2022. She realizes the "race is given to one who endures to the end." Tereon loves the Dallas Cowboys and traveling the World. She wants to build a homeless shelter to help restore hope to the homeless. Tereon believes in helping one person daily to persevere through life.

Hidden Gems
By Crystal McKinley

"You are a palace of hidden gems; the greatest treasure you could ever find is already within you. Gold will melt, money will burn, but you carry the everlasting and mysterious breath of God inside of you, and that can never be taken away."
– A. Helwa.

I have come to realize, in my short time here on earth, that being hidden is a blessing. I realized that later in life. It's so easy to fall into the desire of wanting to be seen when you feel like you're left out. That's a basic summary of my life.

I was born a twin. I love my sister, and we are best friends, but I didn't have an identity outside of 'twin.' People saw 'us' everywhere we went but didn't see me. Because I was soft-spoken and didn't often speak, I was never actually called by my name. I didn't realize how that made me feel until I got older.

For a good part of my life, I felt overlooked and hidden. At times, I even felt buried. My mom was a single mother, my father was nowhere around, and we lived at my grandparents' house with some other aunts and uncles. There was ALWAYS someone in the house. I can laugh about it now because I understand that is how some families were. But it was a lot of people. All the time.

We often had family gatherings, so everyone was at my grandmother's house. It's easy for a sensitive, soft-spoken child to get lost in that crowd. With little attention from my mom and often being left to my own devices, I grew up thinking that's just how it was. I would watch television and see families like the ones on The Cosby Show, only to wish my family was that wholesome. To have a father who saw me and encouraged me.

I had six uncles and a grandfather in the house, so one would think that I had enough male influence and encouragement, but no. We were just kids on the way to my uncle's. We were the babies to my aunts, and I knew my grandfather loved us, but he showed it in his way. I lived in the era of 'be seen and not heard,' so on top of being soft-spoken, I was told not to speak.

It was easy to get into things with no real supervision, and I was exposed to pornography at a very young age. I was hooked and didn't know it. In my eyes, that's how a woman was to get the love and attention from a man. I didn't realize how those images shaped my perception of relationships.

I had to hide from my mother the fact that my sister and I were getting teased in middle school. By high school, my self-esteem was nonexistent, so I just walked the halls like a shell of myself. I didn't know who I was. I remember feeling like my identity was being hidden from me for some reason. All these feelings of being hidden and overlooked came to a head in my senior year of high school.

I wanted what everyone else was getting: attention. I traded in my baggy clothes, because I was a tomboy, and began wearing more form-fitting pants and tops. I was still too shy to talk to a boy, so I practiced on the AOL messenger chat. Most of those conversations were inappropriate but fed into the images that caught my eyes years before.

Eventually, I lost my virginity at 18, opening a new world. I lived on campus for college, but I had sense enough to be selective about who I was in a relationship with. I was prepared to be the most loyal and faithful girlfriend ever, hoping to one day become someone's wife, but much of what I thought was ill-guided. No matter how hard I tried to find a guy, I felt I was still not being seen. It frustrated me!

I wouldn't dress with all my goods hanging out, but I would wear tight jeans and nice tops to get attention. I was saying everything a young college boy in heat wanted to hear, but I still couldn't get a man to pay attention to me. I was 'too nice' or 'motherly.' One guy even told me I was too peaceful for him and needed someone with a little more fire in them.

I didn't know it then, but I can see now how God was blocking the people and things that weren't for me. But I persisted. Eventually, I got into a relationship I knew the Lord was telling me not to get into, and I got pregnant. I didn't know what to do. I couldn't tell my mother or stepdad that I was pregnant and was wasting the money they were paying for my college education. I was scared.

Remember, my mother was a single mom and, by this time, very religious. I had aunts who were single mothers. I knew what it was like and didn't want any part. I did the only thing I knew to do. I got an abortion. The clinic made it seem normal, but I was emotionally torn from the whole thing. I went back to my apartment feeling such guilt and shame.

I wanted to be hidden. I tried to sweep everything under the rug and pretend nothing ever happened. I wanted to put the covers over my head and sleep my time away. But I couldn't. I had to wake up every day and come face to face with a decision I never wanted to make. I was broken. My parents didn't find out until many years later.

The mental despair was too much for me to handle, and my relationship took a turn for the worse. I had to come home. I felt like a failure. I was buried under the dirt of other people's expectations of me. I was fighting against the pressures of people pleasing. My mother wanted me to go to college, but I didn't see that for myself. Some family openly expressed their disappointment and wondered why I didn't measure up to others. I didn't realize we were walking the same mile.

Depression wasn't the word for it. I was empty, but I did what I knew to do: I buried the thoughts and feelings and kept things moving. That was something I had seen modeled for years. We don't talk about what's happening; we bury it and continue to live. But I was dying and didn't know it.

By the time I thought I got things together, I was in another relationship and got pregnant again. I had learned my lesson from the first pregnancy and was adamant about giving birth. I always wanted to be a mother; I just wasn't specific on how that would happen. My son was born, and everything changed for me.

All of a sudden, I had a reason to live. My son didn't ask to be here, but I had sense enough to know that he was a gift from God. It was hard, especially after becoming a single mother. I had to fight every day for the strength to carry on because I wondered how my life ended up like this. I came from a good family. My mother worked her way up from a secretary to an executive director at a major national airport. Technically, I was her firstborn (remember, I'm a twin), so I was looked at to follow her success. But my life was a mess.

But that's what happens when you remove a diamond before it's truly formed. Being hidden isn't a bad thing. Sure, being overlooked isn't fun, but it's often the protection of God. We just aren't in the position to see that yet. I was hidden, but I didn't know the purpose. Precious stones don't need to be handled; they must be cared for properly to maintain their shine.

I was a hidden gem, but I didn't know my value. I didn't speak because I didn't realize I had a voice. I knew I was unique because I could understand things a certain way or see something not many people noticed. But I figured everyone could do that. It's just like the enemy to make you think that those things that make you unique and special are common. No, they aren't!

By the time I came to DIVAS, I was raped twice. The first time, I thought it was my punishment for the abortion, and the second time, I thought it was because I didn't truly deserve to be married or happy. I didn't trust myself. I knew God but I was just starting to develop a relationship with Him. On the morning calls with the DIVAS, I would weep as I sat and listened to women I didn't know share their experiences in life and relationships. I heard my story in theirs. As soon as I began to share my story, God began to heal my heart. Of everything! The prayers of the righteous do avail much.

Let me tell you this.

Your story is my story. You are not alone in this, and it's just like the enemy to make you think you're damaged and should be discarded. It's just like the enemy to make you think that being overlooked means you're undervalued. Hidden gems don't lose their value. They are more valuable to those who can appreciate their beauty.

We all have something that God has put on the inside of us and has hidden us for the right time. If we are revealed too soon, we might be handled by the wrong people, as was my case. Sis, don't let the pressures of life make you want to give up. Diamonds are shaped by pressure. Some gifts must be cultivated in darkness to be appreciated in the light.

Everything you've gone through makes you unique. Every trial has shaped you, and there may have been some relationships that may have cut you. But that doesn't mean your value has diminished. The Almighty God who holds you in His hands determines your value.

Things may seem dark. You might feel overlooked in your job. You might be undervalued in your relationships. But God is working on your behalf! God is a master at taking broken things, making them beautiful, and placing valuable gifts in the right hands. Understand that you are precious in the sight of God. He loves you so much and is bringing you out of that place of obscurity so that you can shine brightly.

Don't lose hope.
Gems are hidden for a purpose.
Precious gems are hidden to be found.

Acknowledgments

I would like to first thank God Almighty. I really would not be where I am without Him.

I would have lost my mind by now. I'm grateful for how God uses my profession as a Health Coach to minister to me and allowing me to minister to others.

I am thankful for my parents, sisters, and family. They have taught me so much about life, forgiveness, and faith.

I would also like to acknowledge my son, Darryl Marcelus, for loving me with the love of Christ and teaching me to receive His love and grace.

DIVAS I love you and I thank God for bringing each of you in my life and pushing me to be where God is calling me.

I have to give honor and recognition to Raylanda McClinton. I know I get on her nerves and she gets on mine, but God has used her to greatly impact my life. I would probably still be operating in hurt and pain if it weren't for her encouragement and prayers. I love you, girl. You know I have your back!!

Crystal McKinley

Crystal McKinley is a speaker, author, business owner and wellness coach with over 10 years of experience. Her ebook Healthier You has helped a number of people lose weight and gain a better understanding of their bodies. In ministry, Crystal enjoys helping others know their identity in Christ.

As a native of Detroit, MI., Crystal is preparing to launch her wellness courses to help women around the world transform their minds and bodies while growing in the Lord. In her spare time, Crystal enjoys ministering to others, writing, reading, and spending time with her son.

Contact Crystal:
Email at <u>cmmckinl18@gmail.com</u>
@crysmichelle85

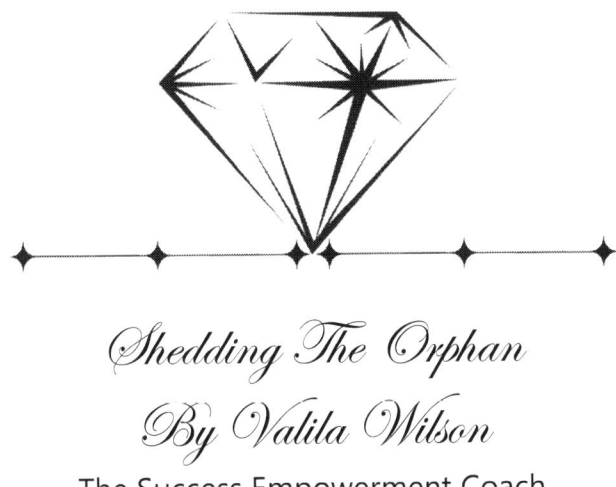

Shedding The Orphan
By Valila Wilson
The Success Empowerment Coach

The Princess and The Hero

The little princess anxiously awaited by the window, peeking out for the big red Cadillac commanded by her hero to charge up the driveway. She wondered why he was taking so long. What was keeping him? Her tummy rumbled and roared. Her mother had generously and lovingly prepared dinner. However, the little Princess was waiting for her hero as usual. She so enjoyed their dinner time together. She would tell him about her day as he sat patiently and eagerly listening. He often stuck his fork into her delicious meal, bantering and teasing her. Sometimes, she would frown and then laugh. Other times, she would just burst out with a giggle of joy. But something kept him, which seemed to be becoming the norm lately. As the sun descended, her mother gently guided her to the table for her meal. She picked up the food with disappointment and sadness, chewing as if in pain. With a nice bowl of ice cream drizzled with chocolate syrup and sprinkled with yummy nuts, her loving and attentive mother did her best to compensate for the hero's absence.

It was time for the little princess to prepare for a night's rest. As her mother rustled the towel about her wet 7-year-old little body, she laughed just a little. Her mother always had a way of cheering her up and encouraging her to move forward despite disappointment. As she climbed into the bed, she heard a Jingle and a jiggle at the side door. She jumped down and ran to the door, and there he was. Her hero had finally come home. "Where have you been? I had to eat dinner without you again." She kissed his cheeks and hugged him so tight. He hugged her quickly and securely placed her back on the carpeted floor. "Okay, now go ahead and go back to bed. I'll see you tomorrow."

With her head hung down, she began sauntering towards her room. As she dragged her feet, she said to herself, "Something is different; something has changed." Since the comfort from the delicious bowl of ice cream had dissipated, she curled up in her bed with her favorite stuffed animal, Scotty, the half-eyed, red-matted fur dog.

As her favorite blanket snuggled her, she continued to think of the lack of warmth and joyfulness from her hero. "Why was he not happy to see me?" Her pillow began to absorb the salty tears from her little eyes. She struggled to understand what was happening. "What have I done? What is wrong?" she questioned as the heaviness of her eyes ushered her into the land of slumber.

Not by the choice of the little princess, she and the hero grew distant as time passed. He no longer called her "kick-a-boo" or "sweet pea." There were no more loving dinners together or fun outings. The hero had become emotionally distant, critical, and judgmental of his once beloved little princess. She became the object of his ridiculing jokes and putdowns. He seemed to love reminding her of how fat she had gotten. See, the little princess learned to take comfort in food. Food brought her pleasure, and for a moment, she would escape the pain of being thrown away and discarded by the one who no longer saw her as special and wonderful, the one who saw her as fat, undesirable, and not good enough to be his darling daughter. There was no more princess and hero, just an 8-year-old, broken-hearted, chubby little girl who had been emotionally abandoned and rejected by her father, who once was her hero. Although she had an attentive and loving mother, she had begun to develop the mindset and attitude of an orphan.

You may wonder if this story is true, but I assure you it is. I personally know the little princess. I would love to tell you that she had no more heartache or struggles, but that would not be true. She endured much hurt and wrongdoings at the hands of others, including her beloved father. This caused her to consistently do things to gain acceptance, approval, and perceived value. She often felt she did not fit in and believed others were superior. Over time, she lacked trust in others as she thought they would inevitably betray her. Due to the constant letdowns from people, she learned to depend solely on herself and her faith in God. She worked hard to gain approval from others, feeling unworthy of love and kindness. She rarely asked for help and pretended to be happy. She would hide her true feelings for fear of being rejected or abandoned. She had learned to portray a particular persona of value and worthiness to fit in and gain approval.

When the charades became too tiresome, she would shut down and retreat. Alone and in great pain, she would self-medicate with her comfort food and escape into the world of Hollywood12` while suffering in silence within her dark cave. Can you relate? Do you see yourself? If yes, be glad and get excited. The enemy has been exposed, and you are no longer fighting in the dark. You can have victory just like the princess eventually did.

The princess had a fantastic support system filled with love and encouragement, with her mother at the forefront. Her mother's unwavering love and belief in her daughter never faltered, even when the princess lacked self-confidence. Her mother pushed her to achieve her best and to exceed expectations. Now a Queen, the princess has transformed into a stunning multi-colored butterfly. She walks with confidence, knowing she is loved and special. The Queen understands she is uniquely made and designed for a particular purpose. She walks in her divine calling and purpose while passionately empowering others to do the same. Who is she? You've guessed it. It is me, Valila, "the little princess," now a Queen and no longer an orphan.

I am blessed and glad to be able to encourage those who relate to my story. You must know that you can be delivered, freed, and healed from the orphan spirit. Over the following few pages, I hope to encourage, inspire, and, most of all, empower you to transform from identifying as rejected, abandoned, and not good enough to feeling and knowing you belong, are loved, and accepted.

The Awakening

The term orphan can be a simple but complex concept. I never really gave it any thought, which is funny because my mom was an orphan and even lived in an orphanage for a short period of her childhood. However, I never thought much about what constitutes an orphan and the effects of their experiences. That is, till one day, I discovered something profound about myself.

While at church one Sunday, I had a personal moment with God during praise and worship among fellow brothers and sisters. I poured out my heart to God because I struggled to understand what was wrong with me. Although I deeply loved God, I struggled to connect with Him consistently. I would get close to Him and then pull away. I was not consistent in my church participation. I recognized that this was not beneficial if I wanted to be utterly devoted to God and unwavering in my faith. I desired a more profound, stable, intimate relationship with God that aligned with His desires for our bond. Furthermore, my relationships with others seemed to be unstable and lacking. Some were even unhealthy and toxic. I felt so alone and unseen. No one seemed to understand the pain of my darkness. I reached a place of just going through the motions. The light I could always find at my darkest moment seemed to fade, and the darkness was about to win until that Sunday. I cannot fully explain the experience of my private time with God, but I now realize it was preparing me for what was to come next.

After Service, out of obedience to God, I approached one of the Prophetess and asked for prayer. When she asked what I needed prayer for, I had no clue but spoke what was on my heart. I shared how I wanted consistency in my church attendance and relationship with God and others. Oh boy, I tell you, God had her to go in deep and war on my behalf. Guess what? She exposed my enemies (of which I was unaware of their presence) and began to attack them at their core. I tell you, when she called their name, I felt something break inside. Every time she would call the orphan spirit and the bastard spirit, I felt as though chains were being shattered. I felt them detaching from my spirit. The prayer was done, but I could not move. Completely surrendered in a sleep-like state, I rested in the chair.

The anointing covered me like a heavy, comfortable blanket as The Holy Spirit continued to work within me. At that moment, I was delivered by the

Holy Spirit and realized a stronghold had been hindering my effectiveness, but it no longer had power over me! I was amazed yet relieved. I gained insight into my struggle and could pray more effectively. Although I had been awakened to the truth of what had bound me, I did not know what it looked like for the orphan spirit to operate within me. I was unaware of when my behavior, emotions, and thinking reflected that of an orphan, but that was okay.

Now that I had been awakened to the truth, I could share it with my community of sisterhood, DIVAS (Diamonds, Inspiring, Virtue, And Success). Through prayer, love, support, and accountability, my sisters would help me fight and walk in freedom because that is what DIVAS does. This had become a community affair. And let me tell you, God showed up and showed out at the DIVAS Experience 2022 in Orlando, Florida.

The Experience

DIVAS has been hosting a women's empowerment weekend at a hotel in southwest Detroit for several years. However, God had given Raylonda McClinton (the visionary and leader of DIVAS) a new vision for 2022. This time, God wanted to go beyond empowering us by giving us an experience that would cause the limits to come off and elevate our faith. He sent us to Orlando, Florida, to stay in a mansion where everything would occur. This was the first time for most of us to have stayed in a mansion. We were provided a personal chef, a heated pool exclusively for our use, and private bedrooms for added comfort. One of the items on our agenda was the daily 5 a.m. prayer; yes, I said 5 a.m. I am not a morning person, and it was a struggle, but I am so glad I was obedient and willingly engaged.

On the second morning of prayer, a few minutes late, I sluggishly shuffled down the stairs and began to pace the floor while praying. After about 30 minutes or so, I felt led to sit down. I got quiet and fell into a sleep-like state. Although my sisters were very present, I wasn't aware. It was as if God Himself physically covered me with the same blank of anointing from my awakening day at church. Fully immersed in the anointing, The Holy Spirit began ministering to me. At some point, with my eyes still closed, I saw a transparent figure separate from my body as if I had shed something like in the movie Ghost. I asked God what was that. He said, "That was the orphan spirit, and you are free. I need you to believe you belong and are my child, whom I love dearly. I adopted you when you accepted my son, Jesus, and my Spirit seals you. No one can pluck you from my hand. I love you, and you belong."

I could only cry a river at that moment while praising and worshiping my Heavenly Father. As I continued to praise and worship, it felt like fire washed over me and moved throughout my body. Unable to contain myself, I began flowing around the room with animated praise and worship. I opened my eyes for the first time after having shed the orphan spirit, and not only did I GENUINELY FEEL LIKE I BELONGED, I <u>KNEW</u> I BELONGED.

Words of Encouragement

Please understand that our sense of acceptance, worthiness, belonging, and unconditional love is not based on others or performance but on our identity in God. Because God loves us, He sent His son, Jesus, to die for us. We do not have to earn his love and acceptance. If we confess with our mouths that Jesus is Lord and believe in our hearts that God raised Him from the dead, we will be saved. When we do this and accept Jesus as our Savior, we are adopted into the family of God. God becomes our Heavenly Father, not to be confused with our earthly Father. This means you are loved and not alone despite your flaws and mistakes. This means you have someone you can trust wholeheartedly. God will never leave or forsake you; you can count on Him. He loves and accepts you. You Belong!

My sister, know that God loves you deeply and desires you to experience complete healing and freedom. I am not sure what your journey may look like. And I am not saying it will be a walk in the park. I could only share bits of my journey, which I am still on. I overcame many mental and emotional struggles and am still working through some with God's help. I am beginning to understand which behaviors, thought patterns, and attitudes stem from an orphan identity. But God is there with me every step of the way. He will be there with you as well.

There are two things I would like to encourage you to do. First, accept Jesus as your Savior and Lord. It is simple. Repeat this prayer, "God, I ask you to forgive me for my sins. I confess Jesus is Lord. I believe in my heart that you raised him from the dead. I receive Jesus as my Lord and Savior. In Jesus Name, Amen." Congratulations and Welcome to the family, my sister. Now that you are a daughter of God, remember that our sense of acceptance, worthiness, belonging, and being loved unconditionally is not rooted in the people around us or our performance but in who we are to God and what that means. You are valuable and now Identify as the daughter of God.

Second, I encourage you to lock into communities of empowerment. If you just accepted Jesus, I recommend you start with a Bible-teaching and Holy Spirit-leading church. Pray to God for guidance in finding the church he desires for you. Ask Him to reveal other communities you should join. It could be an organization or a group gathering for a common cause. Empowerment communities can take many forms, including social, professional, personal, or political. We all need supportive communities that empower us for success, providing accountability, growth, opportunities, increase, and fellowship.

Look how God moved through the communities of my church family and my DIVAS sisterhood to help me get free. I have been blessed to have a professional community that has greatly helped my business. My communities of empowerment were very instrumental in my victories and success and still are. And for you, community is just as vital for your well-being. I understand it can be difficult for you to trust others due to past disappointments and betrayals. I know that rejection can be a frightening and hurtful experience. I understand you prefer to keep a distance from others and value your independence. My sister, I must tell you that God designed us for community. Contrary to popular belief, we are not designed to thrive alone for long periods. We are created as relational beings. It is imperative you understand, my sister, that we need each other, and we need to actively belong to not just a community but a community of empowerment.

For free downloadable prayers to assist on your Journey, visit successempowerment.coach.

Acknowledgments

God, I thank you for your grace and that it is sufficient. Thank you for being the master orchestrator, and I can be confident that all things work out for my good because I love you and am called according to your purpose. Thank you for your unconditional love for me and that I belong. Thank you for securing and adopting me into your family. You are eternally my Heavenly Father, and I love you, Abba Father.

Mom, your unwavering love, acceptance, and belief in me were an anchor and the fuel I needed to rise above my pain and trauma. You empowered me to be the best version of myself and always to do my best. Although you have gone home to be with our Lord, you are still here with me. All the moments shared, lessons taught, and certainly, your famous phrases will forever be a part of my soul and spirit. " Where there is a will, there is a way; There is more than one way to skin a cat; Always go the extra mile." (**Janie May Pugh, Wilson**) I love You, Mommy.

Dad, no matter our challenges, I will always be a daddy's girl. I am grateful for the privilege of spending your final two years with you before you went home to be with the Lord. It was truly an honor and a blessing. Because of our final time spent together, I learned to let go of who I wanted you to be and to accept you for you. We made our peace, and I landed in a place filled with forgiveness, love, and understanding. "Time don't wait on nobody; Money don't grow on trees." (**John Daniel Harris**) I love you, Daddy.

Thank You, **Prophetess Beverly Jordan,** for your obedience to God. Thank you for exposing the enemy and going to war on my behalf. You told me I belong and no longer have to run and hide. I will forever be grateful for your gifts, anointing, love, and support. I love You.

All my **DIVAS Sisters,** I Love you and am honored to be doing life with you! We are taking the limits off, breaking chains, and reaching greater heights in God. Remember, "No shame on you, shame off you." (**Coach Raylonda McClinton**). I love you, Coach.

Valila Wilson

Valila Wilson is a powerhouse of skills, experiences, gifts, and passion that converges into her life mission as a Transformational Success Empowerment Coach. She has a B.A. in Psychology, a business management certification, and is a John Maxwell Certified speaker, coach, and trainer.

As a visionary with 40+ years of leadership experience in ministry, business, coaching, counseling, training, and entrepreneurship, Valila is establishing a legacy of empowerment that adds significant value to the people and communities she serves. She is an international multi-bestselling author and the founder of Essentially Beautiful Women's Ministry, Creations By Design, and Success Empowerment LLC.

Valila has dedicated her life and believes her divine purpose is to empower individuals and organizations to go to their next level, finish strong, obtain sustainable success, and thrive. Ms. Wilson's transformational approach strategically focuses on personal, professional, and leadership development centered around the empowerment of mindset, skills, and tools necessary for going to the next level and soaring to better heights.

Contact Information:
successempowerment.coach
valila@successempowerment.net
Instagram succesempowerment.withvalila
Facebook Pages: Success Empowerment LLC
YouTube: Success Empowerment With Valila

God Is The Healer of My Scars
By Angelina Rideaux

"It's time to let go and let God step in!" Ephesians 3:20: let go and let God have his way in your life, and he will bless you exceedingly abundantly above all that you can ask or think. For years, I blamed God for putting me through the storm. I can Remember Me telling my grandmother: "What's the use of praying when bad things keep happening to me?" I couldn't understand God's plan or purpose for me. I didn't think I had a purpose in life because everything I went through, from childhood to adulthood, was a bad experience. I felt that God didn't love me. I thought to myself, if he did, he wouldn't have given me a life full of pain. So, I thought.

Before coming to the Divas, I was trying to figure out life. I had just lost my job of 7 years (2019). A few years before, CPS removed our kids from the home for 5 months. With all this going on, with the loss of my job and being arrested on theft charges, I felt like I couldn't take any more. I wanted to give up and throw in the towel. And I asked God to take my life. I told him I didn't want it if this was how my life would be. I was tired of hurting. I was tired of going through the pain. Haven't I had enough? Being abused. Being raped and going through different emotions as a teenage mother. How much can one person take?

At this point, I didn't know what to do. I didn't know which direction to take. I didn't know if I was on the right path or not. But one thing I did know was something had to give. Something had to change. I had to learn how to listen. I had to change. I had to allow God to step in. And take control of the things that I didn't have control of. I had to learn how to let go. And that is the hardest part any person can do is learn how to let go and forgive the ones who hurt them.

At the end of 2019, going into 2020, I rededicated my life back to Christ. I knew I had to find my way back and build a relationship with him again. I told God to show me the right way to bring teachers and mentors into my life that he wanted. He told me I had to change something in my life. I had to be obedient to his word. I needed to rethink the people I had in my life. It was challenging to break my old ways. My husband introduced me to the clubhouse in November of 2020. He wanted me to learn how to trade and found a modern black Girl in the Clubhouse.

When I became a member of Clubhouse, I didn't know what to expect. As I learned how to navigate Clubhouse, I wanted something more. I wanted to find a group of women who were God-fearing women. Who are encouraging and inspiring. Currently, I am in the process of changing my mindset and my circle. I could hear God say to me keep searching. Your sisters are nearby. One morning, I found myself going in and out of different rooms. I came across Wake, Pray, Slay, and Command Your Day with the DIVAS. Listening to the divas and the other sisters testify made me look at life differently than I did before. I found myself coming into the room every morning at 5:45 AM. My spirit was moved in a different way that I couldn't explain. I would go into the clubhouse room and sit and listen to the sisters tell their testimonies, their experiences in life, and what they were going through every day. I knew God had a plan. I knew right then, and there I found my tribe. The Divas taught me how to pray and build a relationship with God. They helped me find my purpose in life. The Divas gave me something that I have never experienced. They gave me a place to belong without judgment.

When COVID hit, my vision became clear. I started to understand God's purpose for me. Things were going in the right direction. I started getting involved in the church. I started networking with different women. My mindset was changing. I EMAILED THEM TO JOIN when I found out the Divas had an organization outside the clubhouse.

I was ready to take the next step but found myself at a standstill. I found myself stuck. In January of 2021, my dad passed away. I had just found out I was pregnant. My church was having problems (fighting, arguing, the pastor stealing money, etc..). The devil was trying me. He was mad because he saw that I was moving. He saw that I wasn't letting anything come in my way or stop me. However, I did find myself slipping after my dad passed; I never went through with the Divas enrollment and stopped attending Clubhouse in the morning. I needed time to think and figure out what was happening and what was going on in my life. I had to understand the direction that God wanted me to go.

With everything going on, I didn't want to fall back into the same situation I was in—blaming God and questioning him about what was happening. We have all heard the saying: "If it's meant to be, God will reconnect you to that person or whatever you were disconnected from. Six months later, God did just that. He led me back to the Divas. He brought the Divas back into my life again because he knew that the Divas were my tribe. The DIVAS was the sisterhood that he wanted me to be connected to. A sisterhood full of women who know the word of the Lord. Who will encourage, inspire, and uplift me?

Once I started understanding God's purpose, God told me to do things. Remember, I said God told me to be obedient. Well, that day came when I had to be obedient. I had to make some sacrifices. The first thing God told me to do was write my book. It's time to tell your truth. In my head, I'm like, God, are you kidding me? I have no money. I have six kids and a husband to provide for. I lost my job. I owed over $29,000 in probation fees and restitution, and you telling me to write a book, I'm like, OK, father. We're going to do this. The crazy thing is that you might think it's impossible, but God sees otherwise. I had to learn to put my faith in God. I had to see things his way and not my way. Luke tells us that with God, nothing is impossible. What I was going through at the time, I had to believe. In July 2021, I released my first book, Truth, No More Secrets.

Life is a mystery. He said you never know what will happen in the Movie Forrest Gump. Quote, "Life is like a box of chocolates. You never know what you're gonna get." If you think about life, it is like a box of chocolate. When you get a box of chocolate, you are excited; you don't know what Flavored chocolate will be in the box. You open it, take a piece of chocolate, and put it in your mouth. Now, you might like it, and you might not. Either way, will you keep eating chocolate until you find a piece you like? That's life. You wake up every day not knowing what the day will bring. But you are excited because God gave you another day to get it right. I want to encourage every one of you to reveal your scars. Embrace your scars. Take the time to start your healing process.

Here are three ways to start your healing journey: 1. Build a relationship with God. Learn God's word. How do you plan to defeat the enemy when you don't know the right scriptures to fight with it? 2. Start researching yourself. This is when you want to face what's been hurting you. You might have to get a therapist. 3. Start the process of changing your mindset. During this process and step three, you want to connect with like-minded people. People who are going to encourage, support, and hold you accountable.

Being a part of the Divas has been amazing. I have learned so much. I have done so many assignments. One assignment came from the Diva's clubhouse, Lady Blue Jays Holding Our Sisters Accountable Planner (2022). I remember one of my sisters from the Divas wanted to be held accountable for being on time to work. God came to me and said create an accountability planner? I'm a best-selling author. I spoke at my first women's conference (2023). I'm in three anthologies. Cover by scars make #3. I have written another book, The Powerful Word of God: Destroying Chains In Our Lives! (2023) It's incredible how your mindset and life can shift if you allow God to work and accept the people he brings into your life.

Scars take time to heal. When I look at my scars, they remind me of my strength and that God has always been by my side. It's a reminder that the enemy tried it but failed. No matter how hard the enemy strikes, I know God will strike harder. I want to encourage everyone to keep pushing forward. Don't allow the enemy to destroy what God has created, which is you. God created each of us for a reason. We all have an assignment to complete. You must get off that couch, step out of your comfort zone, and allow Jesus to be your light through the darkness. Ask the Holy Spirit to guide you in the right direction. Remember, giving up is not an option.

Acknowledgments

I must give all glory and praise to my Father God for making all this possible. To the love of my life, Reginald Rideaux, thank you for always supporting me during this incredible journey. Thank you for always believing in me and never doubting me. Raylonda McClinton, Queen, you are a blessing to me. I want to thank you and the Divas for accepting me. Never judging, always supportive. It was your obedience to God's instructions that made this anthology possible. God has major plans for you, sis. Keep pushing through. Tashanna Richardson, you have always been supportive and encouraging. You push me out of my comfort zone. You help me find my purpose. You were the first to reveal what true sisterhood is about, and I thank you for that. Amanda Ashford, you have always been a true sister and friend. From day one, you've been there. We've been through so much together, and I want to say I love you. And thanks for always showing up. Tia Monique, God knew what he was doing when he placed you in my life. Thank you for helping me complete my assignments. To my fantastic mother, Cassie Mitchell, thank you for loving me.

Angelina Rideaux

Bestselling Author Angelina Rideaux is a woman of unwavering faith; she passionately serves as the President of the Women's Missionary at Springfield Baptist Church, where she leads with dedication and purpose. Her mission is to inspire, encourage, and empower women to live in their truth and lead them to Christ. Angelina's transformative journey is vividly chronicled in her book "My Truth No More Secrets," a testament to her resilience in the face of adversity. Beyond her personal triumphs, she passionately empowers fellow Christian women, guiding them to share their stories and transform pain into purpose in just six months. Angelina continues to inspire with upcoming releases like "The Powerful Word of God," slated for September 1st, 2023. Her literary contributions extended to two anthologies such as "My Life As A Girl Boss" and "Making Moves and Not Excuses 2-year Undated Planner." Angelina's creative prowess shines through in the "Lady Blue Jay Holding our Sisters Accountable Planner," a meaningful creation available on Amazon. As the visionary Founder of Rideaux's Expressions, Angelina is steadfastly committed to inspiring, uplifting, and guiding women toward embracing their authentic selves and finding solace in their faith. Angelina is a resilient mother of six, grandmother, and devoted wife for over a decade; hails from Austin, TX, and currently resides in Rockdale, TX.

Contact information:
Social media
Facebook/ Instagram: @authorangelinarideaux
Tiktok: @mrsrideaux67
Youtube:@authorangelinarideaux7666
Email www.angelinarideaux@rideauxsexpressions.com
www.angelinarideaux@gmail.com
website www.rideauxsexpressions.com

Unbreakable
By Dr. Tiffany Moore-Mellieon

"Jesus!" I exclaimed after dropping my wedding ring. I'd just walked in from work and usually went straight to my jewelry box to put my ring up. Instead, I started talking to my husband. I was talking and playing with my ring when it slipped off my finger. For a hot second, I panicked as if my diamond was breakable! I knew better. After all, diamond derives from the Greek word "adamas," which means unconquerable or indestructible! I was quickly reminded that though we may get dropped, we are unbreakable! Apostle Paul said it this way, "We are troubled on every side, yet not distressed; we are perplexed, but not in despair; persecuted, but not forsaken; cast down, but not destroyed;" (2 Corinthians 4:8-9 KJV)

Whew! I can truly attest to this scripture! Lord knows I've been through the storm and rain, but I'm so glad I made it! I've been bumped and bruised. I may even have some scars, but my scars tell a story! They are a road map of my life. They illustrate my journey. You see ... my scars are not a reminder of what I went through but my testimony of what God brought me through!

Imagine being a teenager dealing with peer pressure, bullying, sexual identity, hormones, school, and trying to find your place in life. That's enough to contend with! Imagine being 13, pregnant, and thousands of miles from your family – from your mother! (Because who doesn't want their mom when pregnant?) Well, that was me!

It was June 1989. I was eagerly awaiting my 8th-grade promotion ceremony. I was a 4.0 student heading to high school with honors. My excitement soon ended when my mom warned me not to attend my ceremony. "If you go to your ceremony, they will take you from me!" I'll never forget those words or the events that ensued. I desperately wanted to be with my friends, celebrating our accomplishments, signing yearbooks, and pledging always to remain close. However, attending my 8th-grade ceremony could be more of a problem than a promotion. I was stuck between a rock and a hard place!

After warning me, my mother left with my younger siblings. I decided to skip my 8th-grade ceremony. I hung my fuchsia dress back in the closet. I retreated to the basement, which had become my living quarters. I attempted to sleep the moment away, but a knock at the door interrupted my nap. Child Protective Service (CPS) and the police were at my door! The inevitable happened. I was taken into custody by CPS, who transported me to a group facility. There, I was questioned about my mom, given a physical, and learned, or shall I say "confirmed," what I suspected - I was pregnant!

You're probably wondering why I was taken from my mother. If you're familiar with the Starz series BMF (Black Mafia Family), you've gotten a glimpse of my life in the 80's. Drug users and dealers often surrounded me. Then, there was the occasional truancy issue and my 17-year-old live-in boyfriend. I can see how this may seem dysfunctional!

My dad and mother's parents conspired to take me from her before, and they were at it again. At the time, my dad battled alcoholism, so he had his demons to fight. I guess it was determined that he was the lesser of the two. I was previously evicted from both my grandparents' homes (and that's a talk show for another day). Here they were, uprooting me from my mom.

Now, I'm in a group home away from my dysfunctional environment. It was not necessarily what I anticipated and certainly not what I wanted! I had to think fast. I needed an exit strategy. Fortunately for me, the Detroit Pistons had just won their championship and were having a parade to celebrate. The group home residents were awarded a field trip to the parade. Talk about timing!

Instead of getting settled in, I was preparing to break out! I decided to fake being ill after breakfast so I wouldn't have to attend the parade. There would be limited staff, which meant limited supervision. I waited for my roommates to leave, made a few passes through the hallway to check for the team, opened my room window, and checked the backside of the facility. The coast was clear! I checked the hallway again, climbed out the window, and ran quickly. Without hesitation, I climbed the fence surrounding the facility and ran some more until I met up with my ride. I was officially a fugitive of the state.

I moved over 2,000 miles across the country from life as I knew it. I was 13, pregnant, and even with my boyfriend's family, I was alone and afraid! I couldn't contact my mother out of fear of being tracked down by CPS. I couldn't contact anyone in my family because I didn't know who I could trust. Talk about scars!

Fast forward to February 22, 1990, I'm now 14 and giving birth to my firstborn! It's a boy! I was still on the run and a high school dropout, but I reconnected with my mother and family. That was one burden lifted, but I couldn't go home yet! The whole CPS situation was still looming over me. Instead of confronting the problem I left in Michigan, I suffered silently – dealing with my boyfriend's indiscretions! I was learning to be a mom, and he was learning to be a playboy. Now, where have I seen this behavior before? Oh yeah ... my dad! I guess the old saying "girls marry their fathers" has some truth, but that's a story for another day.

I was in an open relationship that I didn't consent to, but at this point, what were my options? Return to Detroit, subjecting my child to whatever CPS had planned for us? Not an option! Then there was my pride. I didn't want to give my dad the satisfaction of being right, especially considering he was partly responsible for my predicament. Before I departed from Michigan, I visited with my dad, who said I was too young to know what love was and that we wouldn't make it! There is no greater encouragement than telling someone what they can't do. That's a dare!

So, I did everything I could to prove my dad wrong, including having another baby! This time, a little girl was born on February 9, 1992. I'm 16 with two children. Attempting to get my life back on track, I enrolled in PIVOT: New Chance, a program for teen moms. I graduated from the program in 1993! Not long after, I was pregnant with baby #3.

My baby daddy's (notice the change in reference) past caught up with him. He was arrested and extradited to Michigan. It was time that I faced my past, so I moved back home just a few months shy of my 18th birthday. I laid low until I officially aged out of the system – saving Michigan some paperwork and me a headache.

After eight years and another baby later (yes, baby #4), I finally let go of my relationship with my children's father. It was heartbreaking, but sometimes things must be broken to heal properly. Another scar!

The broken pieces of my life were finally coming together. I'm 20 and a single mother of four! I was living life on my terms. After being suffocated for years, I could finally breathe. I was in pursuit of happiness, self-worth, and love!

I endured challenges as a single parent, but my mom was a great help. She afforded me many liberties ... I guess, making up for lost time. I worked, sometimes, two jobs. I partied and ended up reconnecting with someone from my old hood. From our "reconnection" came baby #5! Again, I found myself making something out of nothing to have a family, only to end up with another disappointment, another scar!

After total separation from family, isolation, a drug charge, an abortion, a personal run-in with CPS, two baby daddies, and five children later, I realized something had to change! I had to change! Scars covered me - scars from childhood, failed relationships, and poor choices!

How could a once straight-A student with all the potential in the world have not one but five children out of wedlock by age 23? How could I ruin my life? How was I ever going to manage with five children? Who would want me now? These were questions I asked myself and others asked me. I had no answers...just tears.

I thought I was living my best life, but it was a charade. Despite my best efforts, I was still a prisoner of my past! I was sick and tired of being judged! I was sick and tired of being looked at with disappointment and for being disappointed! I was sick and tired of the silent whispers and the secret mocking!

I lived the street life, hustling and selling drugs. I tried the family thing. I partied like a rock star. I loved, and I lost. None of that completed me. None of it satisfied me. None of it brought me joy.

I started a great career in banking. My children were healthy and growing. I had some struggles, but we were making it. Yet, I was unfulfilled! There was an undeniable void in my life. I was covered by scars – inside and out!

Pregnant with baby #5, I visited the church where my daughter attended daycare. (I would normally attend my grandparent's church, but my car was down.) I experienced God's presence like never before. I found what I'd been missing! I gave my life (for real) to Christ on September 27, 1998, and I never looked back.

I'm not saying the road has been easy. My faith journey presented its share of trials, but God's grace is sufficient. When people saw a broken little girl on a path to nowhere, God saw someone worth saving! He turned my scars into stepping stones, wounds into wins, and pain into purpose! *He has made everything beautiful in its time.*

Some of us don't know who we are without our pain! We must allow the Holy Spirit to heal us from the inside out so we can unearth the diamond buried in the coal – covered by our scars! We are not the sum of our pain or our past. We are not our scars!

My story is not over! This is just a small chapter in my book. Don't allow what you went through to be the end of your story when it was meant to be a bend in your story. It's a comma, not a period!

Where am I today? My parents and I grew through our challenges and have an amazing relationship. I am married, and my husband is truly a God send. I have six loving children and nine beautiful grandchildren. I recently completed my doctorate and have a rewarding career. The enemy tried it, but God denied it! The devil wanted me to lose my mind, but God wouldn't allow it! He sought to kill me, but God kept me!

Now, I am a wife, mother, pastor, therapist, and so much more, but beyond all that, I am unbreakable! All glory be to God! My life is in His hands!

"But as for you, ye thought evil against me; but God meant it unto good, to bring to pass, as it is this day, to save many people alive." ~ Genesis 50:20 KJV

Dedication

I dedicate this project to my mother, Pamela Bolton, who epitomizes being unbreakable! Because of you, I know strength! Because of you, quitting was never an option! Because of you, I am who I am today! To every person who has ever been scarred ... do not conceal your pain; be healed of your pain!

"The very things that held you down are gonna carry you up and up and up."
~ Timothy Q. Mouse (Dumbo 1941)

Acknowledgment

I could not have completed this without the love and support of my family and friends! Thank you, husband, for making my life better and not more complicated. To my children and parents, thanks for being my biggest fans. Thanks to my overseer, Apostle Dr. Keith Richard, for the continual wisdom poured into me and my supportive church family, Elevate Church of Baton Rouge! A very special thanks to my cousin-sister, Raylonda McClinton, for including me in your vision and our sisterhood - DIVAS (Diamonds Inspiring Virtue And Success) for the push and pull. I got my tribe, y'all, and I am truly grateful for that!

In loving memory of Robert "Bob" Evans, Apostle Dr. Kenneth E. Bolton, Sr. and Barbara Bolton, Ernest H. Johnson, Sr., and Marie Hensley-Polk!

Dr. Tiffany Mellieon

Dr. Tiffany Mellieon, a native of Detroit, Michigan, is a Licensed Professional Christian Therapist, Certified Master Life Coach, Motivational Speaker, Master Conference Moderator/Facilitator, and Entrepreneur. She is a God-fearing woman and ordained Pastor who has served in various capacities of ministry for 25 years. Dr. Tiffany is the proprietor of Moore To You, LLC, and founder of Girl BYE (Be You Exceptionally). She is also a founding member of Diamonds Inspiring Virtue and Success (DIVAS) and an advocate for women's empowerment. Dr. Tiffany endeavors to help anyone she encounters become their most exceptional self, but she's especially passionate and empathetic towards hurting women and girls. Dr. Tiffany firmly believes in making oppositions opportunities through realized expectations! She is a true Revivalist and an igniter, producing a specific level of heat to reveal the hidden jewel in all she meets! She currently resides in Baton Rouge, Louisiana, with her husband. She is the mother of six children, "MiMi" to nine grandchildren, and an encourager to many!

Phone: 248-310-4174
Email: DrTiffany@MooreToYouLLC.com
Facebook/Instagram: @iamtiffanym Tiktok: @coachtiffanym Website: MooreToYouLLC.com

From Tragedy To Triumph!
By Zina D. Crosson

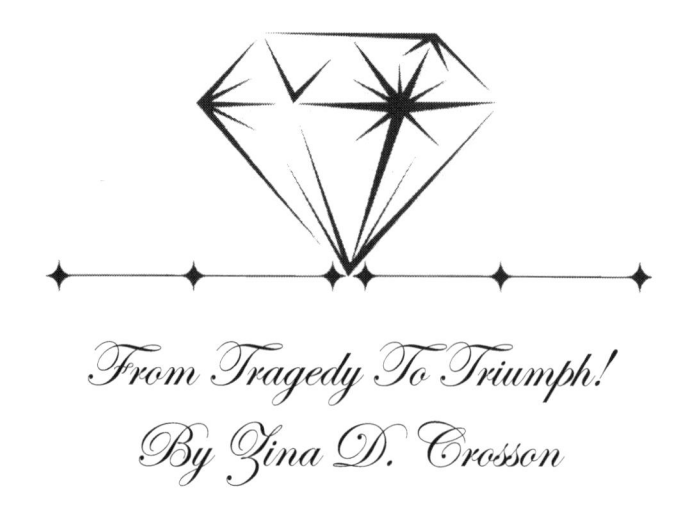

This chapter is dedicated to my angel, Shanee' Shantinique (My Sha-Sha, My Nae). She left me too soon. However, she is watching over me, assuring me that she's okay, and motivating me to go on. She will forever live in my heart!

The Tragedy

December 29, 2018, was the most devastating day of my life. It was the day that my daughter Shanee's heart stopped. On this day, my family and I were at the hospital standing in faith for my daughter's healing when we were told by the doctor, "We're sorry; we did all that we could, but your daughter didn't make it." What's so ironic about this situation is thirty-two years and six months earlier, in this same hospital, I heard the words, "It's a girl!"

I still visualize the three doctors walking down the hallway to deliver the horrifying news. My family and I stood numb and in disbelief after five long days of visits, praying to God, consulting with doctors, witnessing mistakes, correcting some of their staff, doubting their capabilities, contemplating moving my daughter to another hospital, and experiencing three unsuccessful procedures. I had no idea what to do, but my first response was to lift my arms and praise God! As I realized that my daughter was gone, thoughts and feelings of anger, doubt, heartbreak, and pain flooded my mind and heart.

Unfortunately, I had to embrace the task of planning a homegoing service. No parent wants to bury their child, as children normally bury their parents in the natural course of nature. At this time, I did not have the resources. However, as a Christian woman, I put my faith in God's Word, which says, *Be careful for nothing; but in every thing by prayer and supplication with thanksgiving let your requests be made known unto God. (Philippians 4:6)* Also, Philippians 4:19 says, *But my God shall supply all your needs according to his riches in glory by Christ Jesus.* God is faithful to His Word and provided for me, utilizing my family and friends. Their support was unimaginable. All thanks be unto God!

On March 19, 2019, while obtaining medical records, I learned that my daughter's hospital had a specialty heart center. I was so shocked that I ran a red light. I thought, "This must be a new facility that didn't exist in December 2018." However, upon completing my research, I realized the specialty center dedicated to treating cardiac patients opened in 2014. As I wept profusely and texted my family, I wondered why my daughter wasn't transferred to the specialty center. This traumatic experience lasted ninety minutes and put me on an emotional rollercoaster.

Over the next few months, my family, friends, church family, and The DIVAS (Diamonds Inspiring Virtue and Success) helped me through the flood of new emotions. In addition, I began to question God while adjusting to my new normal, helping my family cope with the loss, returning to work, and resuming my service responsibilities at my church. I asked the Lord questions, such as, "Why didn't You answer my prayers? Why didn't You save my child? Why didn't You heal her heart? Is she with You?" I needed answers, and He began to answer my questions one at a time. He said, "I did save Shanee' and gave her a new heart; a heart for me! Shanee' called on Me, and I rescued her! You may not understand everything, but I couldn't leave her there, trust Me!"

As time progressed, God gave me three dreams about Shanee', revealing that she is alive and happy, living with loved ones and her Heavenly Father. Hallelujah! After these dreams, God instructed me to forgive the doctors, the medical staff, the hospital, and myself! He promised me that when episodes of sadness would try to overwhelm me, they would not last long. Truly, I can testify that God is a Promise Keeper!

The Assignment...Journey to Healing

In September 2019, God showed me that there was a purpose in my pain! He woke me up at 3:00 a.m. one morning and assigned me to begin a group for mothers who had also lost a child. I immediately began to give God several excuses. While explaining why I wasn't fit for this assignment, He gave me the truth! He said, "There is purpose in your pain. You are my child, a woman of great strength, an overcomer, an encourager. You are anointed. You have my grace. My Spirit is upon you; therefore, you have great power. You love people. I will give you wisdom, peace, and comfort to share with others to draw them to Me. Together with other women, you will heal!" (Luke 4:18)

Although I initially wrestled with starting the group, I eventually said yes! As I sought God for direction, He gave me the name of the women's group, ***Let's Heal Together***. The vision for the group is as follows: *To develop a sisterhood for ladies who have lost a child, to receive comfort, peace, and healing at any stage of grief.* The mission is *to provide a safe, non-judgmental, and confidential space for mothers experiencing grief, to heal and help others heal by giving and receiving support with empathy and understanding, and to help others to push past the pain and pursue their purpose.* The foundational scripture for *Let's Heal Together* is found in 2 Corinthians 1:3-4: *Blessed be God, even the Father of our Lord Jesus Christ, the Father of mercies, and the God of all comfort; Who comforteth us in all our tribulation, that we may be able to comfort* *them which are in any trouble, by the comfort wherewith we ourselves are comforted of God.*

Our first monthly in-person group met in November of 2019, and continued to meet through February of 2020. Then, unfortunately, COVID-19 shut the world down. As a result, the group had to shut down in-person meetings.

Staying the Course...The Triumph

In October 2022, *Let's Heal Together* began its first online monthly group! To date, the group has in-person and online meetings where roughly a dozen women have been strengthened, encouraged, inspired, and comforted! The women meet regularly to fellowship together by attending jazz and comedy shows, movies, dinner, shopping, and honoring their children's death anniversaries and birthdays. Also, I endeavor to help grieving mothers heal by distributing grief gift baskets, visiting and praying with them, sending flowers, and supporting them during their child's funeral and homegoing process.

Below are several testimonials from the mothers of Let's Heal Together:

The group "Let's Heal Together" was formed when I needed it most, one year after my son's death. As I shared my experience with Zina, she understood what I was going through because she had also lost a child around the same time. I thank God for her obedience because just knowing and being able to share what I go through as a grieving parent has helped

me tremendously. I've learned that I'm not alone; with God, WE can and will get through the pain of grief together. Thank you, Zina!
- Rachel

"Let's Heal Together" has allowed me to share my heart with like-minded sisters. The pain of losing a child is so intense that I feel handicapped at times. As I listen to others, I know I'm not alone, and Jesus walks with us through this journey. I want to help others by sharing my thoughts, experiences, and feelings as I grow into my new normal as a mother without one of my sons. This group is good and helps me as I continue to work through the challenges of grief. Zina is a compassionate person who loves God and people and demonstrates it in this ministry. Thank you for your obedience, Zina!
- Del

This healing group, designed to help women who have lost a child, has done exactly that for me. The women in this group are remarkably free to express whatever thoughts, feelings, and communications necessary to help with the unimaginable! Also, interacting with others experiencing similar loss helps me understand I'm not alone and that it's normal and all right to grieve the loss of my child. Thank God for "Let's Heal Together."
- Ena

Being a part of our healing group has shown me that LOVE still exists in a society that doesn't seem to care anymore. Thank you for sharing yourself and inspiring others to pay it forward to assist mothers in the healing process.

- Alishea

I give God glory for what He is doing in the lives of the mothers. My pastor's sermons, my DIVAS and Clubhouse sister's inspirational words, and the mother's testimonies challenged me to pick up the mantle God gave me in September of 2019 and continue *Let's Heal Together*. As a result, the group is growing and expanding its reach in helping more grieving mothers.

To any mother who has lost a child, may the words below help you overcome the pains of grief and see the future in a brighter light.

"This winding road that we're traveling, the journey of grief, is one of the most difficult to navigate. But, with the love, understanding, acceptance, and growth experienced in *Let's Heal Together*, we will persevere and eventually reach our destinies, a place of peace, comfort, joy, and purpose. So, mothers, don't give up! Our babies are resting with our Heavenly Father, watching over us and cheering us on! Run your race, fight the good fight of faith, and remember ... *Let's Heal Together*"!

Furthermore, I have four points for you to remember:
1) Develop your relationship with God (Proverbs 3:5-6)
2) Don't do life alone; find someone to talk to (Ecclesiastes 4:9-10)
3) Find purpose in your pain (Jeremiah 29:11)

4) In seasons of discouragement, ask God for endurance to continue (Galatians 6:9, Romans 15:5).

In closing, a relationship with God where you experience His supernatural power is crucial in recovering from loss, especially the loss of a child. When you have a relationship with Him, you can see pain through God's sovereignty rather than through the lens of suffering. Know that God is in control and recognize that all tribulations have the potential to glorify Him! I pray that my segment in this anthology gives hope to every mother and reminds them of God's Word, His love and power, and His unwavering faithfulness to us all despite the circumstances we may bear.

Prayer

Lord, You alone are the Healer of our broken hearts. Turn our mourning into dancing and our sorrow into gladness. When we want to give up, push us forward and give us the strength to continue. Please help us survive what we wish we never had to face. I pray that we can do all things through Christ, which strengthens us (Philippians 4:13). I pray that we all trust your purpose, which is greater than anything we could imagine. And we know that all things work together for good to them that love God, to them who are called according to *His* purpose (Romans 8:28). Lastly, I pray that we are used to display your glory and to point others toward You, in the AUTHORITY of Jesus, AMEN!

Acknowledgment

I'm extremely grateful to Minister Raylonda McClinton for the opportunity to share my journey. I acknowledge the Holy Spirit for giving me the strength and the words to write. I thank my husband, Jim, for encouraging me to be an author and being there for me every step of the way. I am grateful to my children and sisters from Let's Heal Together for continuing on this journey of healing with me and always offering a listening ear. I am indebted to my DIVAS sisters for praying and inspiring me through words and deeds, which propelled me to never give up on serving others. I appreciate Minister Marvin and Evangelist Marie Diggs for their love, trust, and support. Lastly, I thank every family member, friend, and acquaintance for praying for me and supporting me in this endeavor. Thank you in advance for purchasing and reading this book. I pray that everyone who reads this book will be inspired to be healed and restored by God! I Love you all. Thank you!

Zina D. Crosson

Zina is a woman of God, a wife, a mother, a grandmother, and an exhorter called to be an evangelist by God. As a result of her servant's heart, she actively serves God and His people through multiple auxiliaries at her local church. She is a leader in SWAT (Soul Winning Attack Team) and in the Ministry Room, as well as a team member at a Women's Halfway House.

In addition, Zina has a leadership position in DIVAS (Diamonds Inspiring Virtue and Success) Ministry, where she inspires and educates women on the most vital subject of evangelism. She also serves as the grievance coordinator for DIVAS members.

Currently, Zina serves as the Executive Administrative Assistant with Marie Diggs Ministries. In addition to serving as an administrator, she also exhorts God's people and helps to spread the gospel of Jesus Christ!

Furthermore, Zina holds a Bachelor of Science Degree in Human Services and is the founder and facilitator of Let's Heal Together, a support group and sisterhood for mothers who have lost a child.

Lastly, Zina and her husband Jim, of eighteen years reside in Detroit, Michigan, along with her children and grandchildren. Her favorite pastimes are spending time with family and friends, traveling, and shopping!

Connect with Zina:
Email: jzcrosson@comcast.net
Facebook: Zina Simms
Instagram: jzcrosson

"The strongest person in the world is a grieving mother who gets up and keeps going every morning." - Tara Watkins Anderson

Blood Diamond
By Marjani Chapman

"I'm here to serve you and only you. Do you get that?"
That's what he said to me.
I'm here to serve you and only you.

Maybe you've heard those words before or experienced a similar love and devotion, but it was MIND-BLOWING for these ears to hear such a thing. I'm not going to lie to you; that one got me. No man, no living, breathing person, had ever said anything remotely close to that about me. Serve ME? ONLY me? My heart and mind reacted instantly. I could feel my heart skip a few beats, then triple in size like that devious green monster in the Christmas movie. I've had plenty of men say all types of things to express their interest in securing a spot in my life, but nothing like this. Unfortunately, instead of receiving and embracing the declaration, I reject it. I dismiss it. He didn't REALLY mean that. Not for me. That was just something to say to get what he wants...

You see, I've always had trouble accepting and giving love. I had the same problem accepting the love of Christ. Something was blocking me, and I didn't know what, but I never felt all the feelings that others felt so easily. The only way I felt valued was by doing. Performing. Executing. Since I didn't feel I had earned my admirer's affection, I couldn't believe it to receive it. Such is the story of my life. Enter Martha.

Introducing "Martha Martha Martha!"

Remember how the middle daughter of the Brady Bunch used to chant out her older sister Marsha's name in frustration? Well, that's kind of how I hear the Lord bellowing to Martha; but not out of middle-child envy. He calls out Martha Martha Martha to chasten and redirect her focus. "Martha" is the author of this chapter. You know Martha, right? She's the sister in the Bible who, when presented with the prospect of Jesus Christ himself and his friends visiting her home, immediately immersed herself into cooking, cleaning, perfecting, and preparing...ensuring everyone was comfortable, their needs were met, and their experience with anything she put her hands to was superb. Martha's dutiful, performance-based, perfectionist spirit is my spirit.

Doing these things is where I see my value, so that's what I focus on—solving, fixing, handling, managing, strategizing, and doing. Standing in the gap, clearing obstacles, figuring things out, and doing. Did I mention doing? Yes, even when it means sacrificing moments to glean and grow and experience the love of The Almighty, I still somehow feel it's more important to tend to the things. The truth is, people pleasing, performing, and appeasing are all spirits that are connected to someone who struggles with self-worth. You can always find me running about doing this or that because it's expected of me, I know how to do it, or I want to be valuable to someone else. If I look at my life today, it's truly the sum of all my yeses. And if I look at my feelings of frustration, disappointment, irritation, insecurity, inadequacy, insufficiency, burnout, checkout, deficit, and so on, it's not hard to see the connection.

I was constantly doing but never accomplishing; constantly going but never arriving; disproportionately giving, pouring, agreeing, accommodating, sacrificing, and leading...all while bleeding.

And so, here I am writing a chapter God never told me to write. A chapter I "felt pressured" to write. I use air quotes for "felt pressured" because the truth is, NOBODY was pressuring me to participate in this amazing endeavor. The offer of authorship was extended to everyone, but I felt no pull towards it. But my inner Martha did. Marjani and Martha wrestled to see who would prevail. COULD MARJANI ACTUALLY SIT THIS ONE OUT? Could she stay focused on her already overflowing plate, or would Martha pick up even more for her to do, because Martha thinks that's what's expected of her as a sister, a leader, and a capable wordsmith. You see, Martha's spirit is the spirit that does what SHE feels is expected of her, even if it was never requested of her. In the Bible, Martha was cooking, cleaning, and working because that's what SHE felt she was supposed to be doing, but nobody TOLD her to do any of that. That very spirit is what I wrestled with.

Yet, here I am, telling this story in REAL TIME, hoping to bless...no, DELIVER the people-pleasing, over-attempting-but-rarely-achieving, performance-based version of us. Yes, US. Because I know I'm not alone, and now you know you're not either. Prayerfully, you've made it this far because you recognize what I'm describing, and you're ready to break free from that spirit and arrive at that happy ending. The happy ending of recognizing your worth and value above and beyond what you can do or earn or achieve. I have not arrived at that happy ending just yet. You've caught me in the middle of a blood bath...a battle between who I've always been and who God created me to be. Thankfully, God has use of every stage of our journey. Miracles in our lives wait until the end to arrive. There are hidden gems being revealed every step of the way. So let's walk this out TOGETHER, and I guess you'll have to buy our next book to continue the journey.

To think I would identify as a people pleaser is CRAZY to me! I used to be so self-centered. I am not selfish, but I am definitely in my head and somewhat oblivious to the world around me. I was always in my thoughts, never looking up to appreciate the present moment or proverbially smelling the roses. I was always thinking and analyzing: trying to figure things out, looking to understand something, or growing my knowledge. It doesn't sound like too bad of a life, except all the while, my relationships with friends, family, coworkers, schoolmates, and the like were all superficial and, frankly, weak. I wanted to have those good, deep, close relationships that many others had...but I couldn't build or maintain those relationships because I was always in my head.

So you would think my mind was a wonderland of dreams, rainbows, and kittens for the time I spent in it, right? Wrong. The truth is, I spent a lot of time in my head because I didn't feel valued, loved, or respected in real life. I silenced and shrunk myself into isolation, spending all my free time picking myself apart and trying to figure out how to be the type of person people wanted in their lives.

Over the years, God has revealed some key characteristics connected to my problem's root. Do any of these sound familiar to you?

1. Insecurity
2. Dismissal
3. Fear
4. Unbelief/Doubt
5. Denial
6. Apathy
7. Stoicism
8. Analytical/Critical
9. Undeserving
10. Lack/Inadequacy
11. Rejection

This list of emotional and behavioral characteristics resulted in me turning inward and not believing ANYTHING good that anyone said about me, even God. Yes, on the surface, I seemed to have a lot of things going for myself. I am intelligent, extremely capable, a fast learner, and hardworking. I have a good heart, am genuine, and only want the best for myself and those around me. And yet, every compliment I have ever received has been met in my mind by skepticism, doubt, and dismissal. If I hadn't DONE something to earn it, I just couldn't grasp it. 'Surely, they were saying that just to be polite,' I would think to myself when the compliment came from a stranger or someone who didn't know me well.

When those closer to me spoke into my life, the battle in my mind became their compliment vs. the laundry list of things they had no idea about that negated whatever they thought was good about me. 'If only they knew!' I would think to myself as I rattled off my most recent failures and insecurities. I couldn't receive it. And that wasn't reserved for people—even God got dismissed! I even spent a season of my life as agnostic because I literally could not understand the love of God.

Then, as He always does when we're out of alignment with His Will for our lives for too long, God turned my life upside down. A devastating end to my only real relationship in life broke me and brought me to my knees. I tried to drink, party, eat, cry, smoke, isolate myself. I tried every toxic solution in the book. Then, after I had inflicted enough self-destruction, I crawled to the throne of Grace. It was time to try God. I still didn't know if I fully understood or believed in the God of my upbringing, but it couldn't be worse than anything else I had tried and failed at. This was the best thing that could've happened to me.

This season, God has been teaching me how much He loves me and how to show love in return. He started with the love of God. He brought Psalm 139:13-14 to life for me. He taught me that everything I listed as flaws that negated any compliment I received was part of my intentional and unique design, which He calls wonderful.

Then, He showed me the love of sisters. As I embraced a life that was all-in for God, I felt more alone and isolated. Then came DIVAS. This sisterhood transformed me from a loner to a leader, from isolated to celebrated. In the blink of an eye, God taught me to love and be genuinely loved. He removed the scales from my eyes so I could see that so many people were in need and that I did have things that could meet those needs. Because of DIVAS, I have grown as a leader, as a sister, and as a person who now thinks about others just as much as she used to think about herself. Because of DIVAS surrounding me, accepting me, believing in me, challenging me to become the best version of myself, and pushing me to do the things I NEVER would've done, I can truly say that I've begun embracing being a Diamond.

Not just a Diamond, but a Blood Diamond. God is healing me from the inside out and allowing me to shine through it all. I'm a Blood Diamond because, though I'm scarred and bleeding, I am still brilliant, beautiful, invaluable, and unbreakable. I realize now why that profession of affection was so impactful to me. It's because it represents the love God has for us. Agape love. Love that loves others as we love ourselves. Love that serves us the way Jesus washed His disciple's feet and spent His life demonstrating the power of God. That's why it truly touched me. It reminded me of the number one thing that makes me a Blood Diamond. I am a Blood Diamond because my Lord and Savior, Jesus Christ, shed His blood and gave his life to reveal my Diamond within.

Marjani Chapman

W hen you hear the name MJ, you immediately think of the G.O.A.T.s (Greatest Of All Time). Michael Jackson, the King of Pop...Michael Jordan, arguably the greatest basketball player in history…and now we can add to the list Marjani "MJ" Chapman.

Marjani is a "people-person," but not the way you'd think. She's a natural communicator, thinker, strategist, and analyst. These gifts have contributed to her professional success as a Human Resources, a leader within DIVAS, and the president and CEO of her consulting business, Transcend Excellence LLC…all of which have enabled her to make tremendous impacts on the lives of people all over the world. And yet, she still identifies as an introvert with extrovert qualities.

DIVAS has been a key factor in the manifestation of God's glory through Marjani's gifts and skills. The organization gave her a safe place and space to be herself, and that unlocked a great deal of potential that has led to public speaking engagements, hosting and emceeing at empowerment events, regularly leading discussions, our drop-in audio podcast space, and so much more.

Marjani is a dedicated mother to her amazing son Aiden, a sister, daughter, leader, intellectual, an amateur crochet enthusiast, and a spiritual seeker. A devoted daughter of God and follower of Christ, she's constantly looking for ways to learn, grow, and be used in the kingdom of God.

Beauty For Ashes
By Sheray L. Laury

No matter what challenges I face in this lifetime, I'm constantly reminded that the things of this world are temporary...it's only an assignment. It's easy to be obedient to God when things are going well in life, but when life starts lifeing, it can become a challenge. One of the biggest challenges I've faced is losing a child. I will reveal how this traumatic loss derailed "my purpose" as I was forced to learn how to process grief while combating mental health illnesses and broken heart syndrome. After God blew a fresh anointing on me, redirecting my steps onto "his path," I realized my true calling. He had given me Beauty for Ashes.

As if 2017 hadn't been bad enough already, a house fire, losing my first grandchild, followed by the death of a grandmother. By the end of the year, I was forced to deal with yet another heartbreak; my son had been involved in a hit-and-run accident and didn't survive it. I remember sitting in my church's front row in the chapel. I stared at my oldest son's poster-sized picture collage that lined the stage in order of his years on earth. Many of those pictures felt just like yesterday. He hadn't been 21 years old for even 90 days, yet his life here on earth was still over. At the repass, I did the same thing: sit and stare at his pictures in disbelief that I, of all people, had just "lost my oldest boy." What had I done to deserve such a thing? He knew Jesus. Had I not prayed hard enough? Was there anything I could have done better? I was confused and lost, with no answers. From that moment, I began "living in my head."

The day after the services, my new reality began. It was still summer, yet the day felt so cold. I was filled with sadness and gloom and obsessed with my son being a memory in my head; I couldn't wrap my head around that. I kept replaying the last time he visited; he hugged me tightly and kissed my forehead before leaving. I felt cheated! I'd flip my pillow over repeatedly after soaking it with tears throughout the day. I hated to see the sun peak through the blinds every morning, to hear kids playing outside or neighbors laughing as they walked by; I hated the sound of people going on with their lives when mine had stopped. It didn't matter that I had three other children who needed me; I was justified in staying in bed, not eating, drinking, or communicating with anyone. I wanted my baby back, and that was impossible. Adding insult to insult, the woman who killed him was only sentenced to 1 measly year in jail. I was devastated! You get to take my son's life away, leave him in the street, and turn yourself in days later for a 1-year sentence. My son's life was stolen, the system had just failed us, and psychosis had crept in without my knowing.

I started suffering from severe depression and anxiety. I no longer had the same joyful and positive outlook on life that I once had. I was so desperate for help that I unintentionally formed a support team around me, including my first lady, church pastor, therapist, and doctor. After my annual physical, my doctor informed me that I had an abnormal EKG and diagnosed me with broken heart syndrome, meaning the left side of my heart was enlarged due to long-term grief after a tragic event. She also disclosed that I could but didn't have to succumb to this sickness as long as I started making some lifestyle changes. I had a new trial to tackle: the battle of mental illness. After weeks of being lethargic as I got used to my prescribed medication, I decided not to allow Satan to steal my mind; I would fight back!

> KJV: Psalm 40:2-3 He brought me up out of a horrible pit, out of the miry clay, and set my feet upon a rock, *and* established my goings and he hath put a new song in my mouth...

I had to learn how to begin speaking "life" over myself, not death. I had to reprogram how I thought and spoke to beat this. The way I see it, it's a disservice for us to get so consumed with the losses we suffer during our journey here on Earth. Whenever I grieve, I feel and walk through the pain: cry, scream, sleep, eat, and whatever serves as a pacifier in that space. There are no shortcuts to grief; walking through it is the only way to get over it. Yeah, I know it's easier said than done, right?! Today, I can say that it's possible, and I believe it. At the same time, it feels like yesterday when I couldn't even see myself engaging in life anymore. Finding the proper therapist can be a process. You may have to try one, 1,2, or even three until you find "a match, " so don't get frustrated. I'm a big fan of therapy; I go bi-weekly and use it as a life coach, but there were many years that I cried never-ending tears on that couch.

A visit with my first lady once taught me that losing our body only ends your assignment here on earth and that you continue to have a spiritual purpose. I learned that time is very slow in the heavenly realm; many years on earth are as one day in the spirit. Therefore, our loved ones don't miss us in the same fashion we miss them; it still feels like yesterday in their minds. This revelation was so awakening for me; it helped me to refocus on my mission. I started thinking, Jaelin is fine; who better to have him between God and me? He'd never want to return to this world again after seeing God.

At the end of all of this, I want God to tell me, "Well done, good and faithful servant," and the only way that was going to happen for me was to tag back in and start the mission that I had aborted when depression had entered into my life. I started filtering the words coming out of my mouth to others, especially myself. I had thought that I'd be depressed and sad forever; hell on earth, this is how my story would end. The biggest lie Satan told me was that I had a "pass" to live in depression and that it didn't matter if I completed my mission because I had suffered this massive loss. God tells us many times in the bible that mourning and grief are only for A SEASON, not a lifetime.

Eventually, God expects us to place our burdens on him so that he can anoint us with his oil of joy. When depression takes root in your spirit, it causes you to loathe and throw pity parties, causing you to spend excessive time thinking about yourself. Walking in your purpose and being self-consumed is impossible because SERVING OTHERS requires you to take your eyes off yourself. You have to MAKE A DECISION to stop living in your head, get back up, and take your life back from Satan and his demons.

The longer you entertain the fabricated story that Satan wants you to believe about your life, is another day that you are not completing your assignment. Your mission was crafted with your unique skills before you were formed in your mother's womb. Satan's goal is to steal your mind so that you can't operate and you're not mobile, which makes you useless for the Kingdom of Heaven. God needs all of his believers to operate with a purpose.

Nothing compares to the loss of a child; the hurt runs deep into your core and feels like a death you participate in in human form. The moment you decide to trust God and agree to be used as his servant, he will fill your void with his love and kindness and goodness and mercy.

I began to rise early in the morning for prayer and meditation to give me the quiet time I needed to speak my heart to God and to allow him to speak to me so that he could redirect my focus and "renew my mind" so that I could stay in tune with his guidance daily, as I began this new journey. I participate in a women's prayer group, which gives me a safe space to connect with other believers and keeps me "covered in the blood" and lifted in spirit. Yoga (online/in-studio) was very beneficial in helping me learn breathing techniques and to calm my anxiety.

I also attend church in person and watch YouTube streamed church sermons as I start my day for extra motivation and to feed my spirit with the Word continuously. If I'm constantly making deposits of the Word in my mind, then I leave no room for Satan to creep in UNNOTICED and start RE-TELLING me the same lies that got me stuck in depression in the first place. I read Christian-based women's affirmation books as a great tool to remind me of God's many scriptures on his promises and how he sees me, encouraging me to view myself similarly. I fast every month or so for a short period to detox and keep my communication line with God clear.

I started journaling and writing down what the Word says over my life; I spoke it aloud, believed it, and stood in faith. I began to see life through a different pair of lenses. I'd take nature breaks to walk through my neighborhood, being mindful to listen to the sounds as I strolled; other times, I'd listen to Spotify podcasts that encourage good mental health practices, which helped to educate while exercising at the same time. I had learned to pay attention to the little things God does that I could be grateful for and eventually replaced my sadness with gratitude. I no longer viewed my loss as a "whoa, it's me" moment. Instead, I say, why not me? What makes me so special that I'm above facing this hurdle? That's all it is: another obstacle I must overcome as I move through life. I'm not the first or the last woman who will experience this type of defeat. There are many of us in this heartbreaking "club"; that is why God prepared his Word to speak to this level of despair. Nothing here on earth can replace the magnitude of God's word in that newfound hole in your heart. The Holy Ghost will comfort you just as he did for me. God put a new song in my mouth, and I began to start a new journey that includes every past version of myself in a new embodiment: I'm stronger, I'm wiser, I'm better! I made it through, and you can too!

Dedication

Dedicated to my eldest son, Jaelin, who was promoted to the heavenly realm in 2017. Because of you, I was re-birthed and redirected to God's portal for me, and I'm walking in my purpose. Thank you for the "gifts" of your spirit that you shared with everyone who crossed your path. You will be forever loved.

Sheray L. Laury

Sheray Laury is not only a wife and mother of 4 amazing kids, but is also the first black female owner of a virtual reality arcade in the U.S. She is Christian and a long-term member of Word of Faith International Christian Center. A Central Michigan

University Alumni, with a Bachelor of Business Degree; coupled with over 25 years of Entrepreneurship, Human Resources, Office Management, Catering & event planning, and cosmetology experience. In 2008, she formed The Party Source Party Rentals, which provides tent packages to clients in southeast Michigan and continues to thrive. In 2017, After the heartbreaking loss of her son, she battled with depression and anxiety for years; but God was still able to use her. In 2019, VR Life was created, a virtual reality center; the first of its kind. Her newest venture includes a non-profit, VR Edutainment, which operates inside of VR Life as a STEAM Lab. It focuses on providing STEAM based experiences using virtual reality, traditional practices, and hands-on experiences to inner city youth; in efforts to encourage them to choose careers in this industry. In 2023, she also designed and launched an online wig store; She by Sheray Wigs.

Email: vrstemedutainment@gmail.com
248-499-7955
Instagram: vr_edutainment
Instagram: shebysheraywigs
Tiktok: @vrlifearcade
Tiktok: @shebysheraywigs
https://www.facebook.com/shebysheraywigs
https://www.facebook.com/vredutainment
https://www.facebook.com/VRLifearcade
https://www.facebook.com/thepartysourcellc

From Victim to Victory: A Story About God's Restoring Love
By Marlo McCoy

Ever since I can remember, I had a dream. A dream of being loved like never before. A dream of how love should feel and look. I dream of being married and having an amazing relationship with a man I can pour out all my love to and feel safe because he sincerely and passionately wants me. I dream of being with someone who feels deeply about kindness like I do. It's a dream to be with someone with only eyes for me. It is a dream to be with someone who can tap into my heart's intensity and hopes and who makes an effort to understand me. To be with someone who believes in love & the power of it, who knows how to handle me with gentle strength. Who supports me and us and wants to live right, live strong, & live with faithfulness, integrity, and trust. To have the kind of relationship that glows with God's light, His closeness, His oneness, and His healthy fire.

I didn't get this dream from watching my parents' relationship because they divorced when I was about five. And, even though their divorce resulted from a breakdown in their relationship before I was probably born, trauma now entered me. My father loved my mother the best he knew how, but the emptiness he felt from childhood, when his mother always favored his younger brother, led to an insecurity within him. Over time, his insecurity led to jealousy; jealousy led to fear and overthinking, leading to selfishness, job-hopping, mistrust, control, and abuse. When my mother (who grew up with an abusive father) recognized this, she wanted him out quickly.

So there I was, living with my mother, who did all she could to provide and show me love while picking up the pieces of her heart. She was willing to look for answers, and in her search, she found Jesus. I also desired to feel love from my dad, but as I got to be a teen, when he looked at me, he saw my mother, who he still loved, missed, and had a broken heart over. I could feel him holding back, pulling away, and gravitating to my younger brother. They had many expressive conversations and interactions, but I felt left out. He didn't appear to have the same excitement with me that he had with my brother. Hence, I felt rejection creeping in.

I wondered, "Is there something wrong with me?" I felt like I wasn't enough, like I wasn't worthy of being loved, and that, somehow, this was my fault.

Thoughts convinced me to settle with this, and as a young woman, I began looking for love in the wrong places. The wrongs were the handful of relationships I entered into that always ended the same way: with me having a heart filled with rejection, sadness, disappointment, & loneliness. Thankfully, I began attending church with Mom, and there was something definitely RIGHT about that.

My pleasant personality allowed me to be easy-going, calm & collected on the outside as if I had it all together. But, simultaneously, I became an expert at hiding my pain. I hid my strong need to fit in and to be confirmed. My deep desire to be wanted and liked by all caused me to people-please, while the yearning to feel special & loved by that particular someone grew stronger.

I wasn't sure who that special someone would be, but I easily trusted, hoping he (plural) had a heart like mine. Time would tell that no one could relate long-term to my genuine sweetness and how I was built to encourage, support, give, & be faithful. These qualities are great in a healthy relationship but detrimental in an unhealthy one. I learned to have a high tolerance for suffering and disappointment.

The pure compassion & sensitivity in my heart got tangled & twisted up with my fears—the fear of rejection, loneliness, and not being enough. And the forgiveness I learned about in The Word of God became my excuse for allowing myself to be mistreated. From 12th grade until my 50s, I had lived with the dark secret of being a victim. Having been cheated on, given a sexually transmitted disease, misunderstood & taken advantage of, lied to & lied on, manipulated, accused, bullied, threatened, silenced, blamed, shamed, emotionally verbally & physically abused, demeaned, defamed, controlled, raped, continually disrespected, stalked, and stripped of whatever minuscule amount of dignity I had left to conjure up a smile still and reply "I'm ok" to the ones who asked "How are you?" in passing.

I thought I knew why I had so much love in me, but as I looked for it to be reciprocated in and from others who couldn't fill that emptiness, I finally had to look within and understand that I didn't love myself. As badly as I desired to be a reflection of my dream, my fear brought imprisonment. I had succumbed to the ultimate low. I was lost—my soul in grave turmoil. My spirit, fighting to grow and learn who I am. I knew I was " saved," and I believed God was watching everything I had experienced. I had worn the mask for so long that I became a functional dysfunction. I was stuck in a cycle of daily breakdowns and a corrupted mindset, crying silently behind closed doors, only to resume life in survival mode. I had reached a breaking point. The point where I was numb and the light seemed so far away in this dark hole. I was finally ready to speak.

"God? There HAS to be MORE to my life than this. Please fix me. I'm damaged, and my heart feels shattered. I believe You can." I knew God had heard my mom's daily intercessions, but had He also heard my mustard seed of faith?

I witnessed God's Divine Intervention occur right before my very eyes. He brought certain people into my life to help inspire me and dig into that hole I was in. Then, quite unexpectedly, God gave me a vision while I was awake one day. He showed me myself lying on my death bed, tears welling in my eyes, stricken with insurmountable regret and deep sorrow & grief. God showed me that if I continued on this path, I would die a miserable death, feeling like I wasted my life away, not fulfilling the call in my heart from Him or living my life to the fullest. This vision confirmed that God has so much more for me!

This vision exploded like a bomb in my spirit so powerfully that it instantly woke the inner warrior. I could feel my spirit rise with courage from all the gospel I had been listening to and digesting for the last 35 years! I spoke out loud, "Oh no! I refuse to go out like that!"

He then gave me instructions, which led me to move out from where I was living, away from who I was living with & into my apartment. God began to perform spiritual surgery on me. My apartment became a prayer closet. He guided me to put scriptures, prayers, and LIFE-giving words all over it.

It was at this point when Raylonda and the DIVAS PRAYERLINE were introduced into my life (Summer of 2019). I called in every morning and quietly listened, quickly recognizing that this was another Divine Intervention from God. These women shared daily devotions, scriptures, life's challenges, encouragement, & prayers, and all of it gave my heart wings! We would read certain books on healing and kingdom authority and have praise and worship. I know first-hand that DIVAS is a safe space to share, a non-judgmental zone, and a place filled with agape love. I belonged there. Nothing is sweeter than knowing that I am exactly where I'm supposed to be.

A very big shift has occurred within me since being with DIVAS. I have a renewed mindset, mountain-moving faith and can hear God's voice. The old me has departed, and a new me is emerging! This is a genuine sisterhood with women who love God, desire to serve, and live boldly for Christ. That's exactly what I want also. Going out with them to feed the homeless, visit transitional homes, host events, collaborate with other organizations, and serve the community has changed my life forever. Doing God's work and doing life together with DIVAS has taken me to another level in God. Some of the life-changing truths that DIVAS has impressed in my soul include:

- Be my unique self because God wants to use me.
- No matter what I have been through, there's no shame on me, but shame off me.
- Prayer works, and my words matter. Align my words with God's Word.
- Find a scripture from the Bible to stand on because there is at least one for every problem we face.

God is Love, and He reminds me daily how much He loves me. His love is the only love that will never fail me. I have learned the proper perspective: God first. His love covers me, strengthens me, protects me, and causes peace that surpasses all understanding. His love has set me on a firm foundation and the right path. His love brings me joy. His love is always with me. His love has mended my heart. His love has healed my body and my mind. I'm no longer looking for love from people like I used to. I no longer fear anything, including what others think of me. I no longer need to fit in but rather be my authentic self and stand out, knowing that God says I am enough, I am valuable, I am marvelously made, and I am created for His good pleasure.

The dream is well and still very much alive in my heart. It cannot be snuffed out because it is God's plan for me to love and to be loved like never before!

Dedication

This chapter is dedicated to my mom, who faithfully prays for the family. I love you. Thank you for praying for the restoration of my life.
To Mashaun and Markell, my children,
I love you beyond words.

To all the women who search for love from a broken place. May you find the Light surrounding you and real Love from God.

Acknowledgment

I want to thank Raylonda McClinton, the visionary of this Anthology and the founder of Diamonds, Inspiring Virtue And Success—DIVAS, for allowing me to be a part of this amazing project.
I love you.

Marlo McCoy

Marlo McCoy boasts an impressive career spanning over two decades within the field of Education, predominantly in the Oak Park School District in Michigan. For a substantial 16-year period, she dedicated her expertise to nurturing children in Special Education who bore labels such as Learning Disabilities, Cognitive Impairments, Autism

Spectrum Disorders, Down Syndrome, and Emotional Impairments.

In addition to her extensive educational background, Marlo embarked on a seven-year journey as a Certified Nursing Assistant (CNA), further solidifying her role as a professional caregiver.

Amidst personal challenges within her marriage, Marlo extended her support by devoting seven years to the SWAP program, an acronym for "SISTERS WITH A PURPOSE," a female mentoring initiative at her high school.

Currently, Marlo stands at the inception of her entrepreneurial venture as a Healing & Transformational Coach, with a specialized focus on aiding abused women in their journey from brokenness to wholeness.

Marlo's path to resilience led her to the realm of martial arts and the art of speed brick-breaking, where she has achieved a black belt mastery in both.
She is a multifaceted artist, excelling as a singer, writer, poet, musician, choreographer, and dancer. Her educational foundation culminated in a Bachelor of Arts in Theatre with a Dance Emphasis, earned at California State University, Fullerton. Notably, she has danced alongside esteemed organizations such as the Alvin Ailey Intensive Summer Workshop and the Los Angeles Clippers Basketball Organization.

Marlo can be reached by email: caligirlmmmm@yahoo.com

Dug Deep
By Brandy Browning

(Sheer determination to come out from where I was buried)

According to a blog from Gloveworx, to <u>dig deep</u> means "to make an effort with all of your resources. Digging deep refers to your ability to look inside yourself, see your potential, and use all you have to reach your goals, live out your values, and overcome obstacles. It refers to your resiliency or ability to bounce back after setbacks."

The Great Piercing

During The 2020 world pandemic, life as I knew it vastly changed. I was well pleased with the trajectory that my life was going. My marriage was amazing, so I thought. We started a relationship at the tender age of 21. I was growing together through our entire 20s, 30s, and now 40s. Things were looking up for us as we followed Christ. Our children were doing great. I operated a successful in-home childcare center; My husband landed a good job in the hospital, which increased our earnings. Financially, we did not suffer as we did in our younger years. We made sure we took the time to date one another on purpose at least once a week. We still prefer one another with no signs of infidelity, abuse, or betrayal. This all changed suddenly! With uncertainty around the world. My business was shut down. Yes, we were side by side, working together to keep our family safe. One month into the pandemic, I was informed of something so devastating that it shook the core of our marriage.

    This cut me very deep; it was like getting buried alive. This is the person that I planned my life with that I saw myself growing old with. We were best friends as well as partners. Once I found out his dirty secret. Which was said to have happened over a decade ago and is now revealed. It's like I Became Public Enemy number one. The man who swore to love, protect, and care for me had betrayed me. I felt like I was being buried alive.

    I began to be neglected and abused daily. Mentally, financially, and inhumanly. I was sexually assaulted on two occasions, the last being the worst as I woke up being pinned to our bed with an unfinished footboard on my throat.

In the Rough

I suffered in silence for over a year. I was separated from my entire family. The world was mostly on lockdown in their homes; it felt like being buried. In the state of Michigan, I am a mandated reporter. So, I reported the incident. And I called the police only to be cut again. By the words of that officer, I cried out for help. My husband was present as I explained to them what happened. My heart was so conflicted. Torn between protecting my husband or reporting was told to me.

My heart was crushed so badly as I looked into my husband's eyes, then he hung his head. This was someone that I, too, was supposed to protect as I chose to do the right thing and stand up for the ones who cannot speak up for themselves.

The officer apologized and said that there was nothing they could do about it because they were over 18 years old when they came forward. I felt helpless! Staying close to God was the only thing that kept me sane. I did not know how I was going to continue to honor my vows to this man. I discovered that not all monsters have grotesque visages and tattered clothing; some wear a suit and tie.

Lifeline

As I was going through this devastating discovery and now mistreatment. I sustained another life-altering experience. Always being a healthy person, doctors advised me that I needed a hysterectomy due to growing fibroid tumors. This means I would never be able to have children, another cut! There were days when I was humiliated after my surgery, having to go public online to ask if someone could come into my home and take the trash out.

As it had piled up and set for days, I was bedridden. I wanted to give up. Yes, I threw in the towel, and it was as if God picked it up and threw it back at me, saying you cannot give something away that does not belong to you. I invited the Holy Spirit into my life to rest, rule, and abide. That I would honor and follow His lead. I trusted him, and I did not understand this matter, so quitting was not an option. It was extremely difficult.

I questioned God for the first time and asked Him, "Why did you allow me to marry him?"

He replied, "Because I knew you would help him."

Not only did I find out the devastating news but I found out that it was a generational curse that needed to be broken. I know that God trusted me with this. I would have never thought in a million years that I would be a victim of domestic violence, although I was not. Physically punched, Sadly, I found myself on "The cycle of abuse wheel" in every other area. Each morning, I used to get on a prayer call with a group of women from all walks of life. I never really had a sisterhood. These sisters were my strength when I was weak. They kept me grounded in God's word. It was a safe place and it helped to strengthen me and remind me who I was in Christ Jesus.

It was a safe place and strengthening. A way to get equipped and reminded of who you are in Christ Jesus.

Local to Detroit, MI, where I reside. These ladies were some of the first to respond to my dire need. It was as if they gave me Spiritual CPR. The longer I suffered, the more difficult it became to stay grounded in God's Word, so I stumbled.

I Fell Hard

I suffered in silence, found a sisterhood to confide in, started counseling, and then met a man. This man came along And showed his concern. While the rest of the world around me seemed not to notice I was going through so much, He could see the pain in my eyes. He knew something was not right. Now I was Proverbial frogged by this man. I was trying to figure out how to get away from the situation my husband started—turning my cell phone off. Putting trackers on my vehicle and following me with a gun.

My husband tried to tarnish my name and say that I was an adulteress and cheating on him after he was told I would not continue this marriage with him refusing to get full council. There was not much else I could do. I was with him for over 20 years, and another man had never kissed me; I was very proud of that, but this man came to me as a protector. He played a major role in helping me get away from the abuse.

As we talked on the phone, one conversation led to another, and it continued. This turned into a full-blown situation-ship. I did not want a relationship; I was crushed! I felt like I had failed God. To make matters worse, this man had previously been married to a relative of mine on my father's side of the family, even though I was unaware at the time. By the time I found out, the stronghold was already set in place. I did not know how to walk away. Now, I dug myself into a deeper hole instead of climbing out. I was removing the base from which I was standing.

Grit

Now, I am walking and embracing the cuts. I felt like my Witness was destroyed; my character had become flawed even though we were now separated after having a personal protection order against my husband. I was still legally married and in a relationship with a very controlling man. The adversary wanted to shame me. He wants us to cover things up. Thinking we'll be ineffective makes for a better witness. Because now you have been through some things, and you can explain them to people. A woman spoke to my mother about me when I was nine years old, saying that I was a diamond in the rough.

When I was nine, God would take your mess and turn it into a message. I learned that sometimes you must be pulled far back to spring forward. You'll go much further at a faster rate. To reveal something great. The Holy Spirit had me study the Book of Job twice. He allowed what I suffered through to be what someone else would need to help them get through and to give them hope.

Know that you are a diamond. A diamond is known for its cuts and clarity. The value goes up. Each cut represented strength, power, and true grit through all these trials in life. The scabs on the scars have been removed, and now I can shine bright, returning to being the world's light.

Tips/what I learned

- The fear may *feel* real but do it anyway. Trust God.
- Seek the answers from God.
- Don't start a relationship before you end the one that you are in. Wait, take time to heal, not to attract familiar spirits. It would be best to have time to heal to know who you are again.
- Forgive yourself; it was not your fault and forgive the person.
- Never give up.

Acknowledgments

With gratitude, love, and appreciation. You were the glue that held me together when I felt like giving up. You make my journey worthwhile. For all mothers. To every wife that has suffered in silence. And to every child who feels like they do not have a voice (you do), it's needed. The one true living God, My Father in Heaven. Holy Spirit. And Jesus the Christ. My mother, Anita Gaddis. My sons Deonté Gaddies, DaiQuan Browning, and DaiSean Browning. My entire family, for there are too many to name, my extended family Tadasia DeBoest, Kammie Anderson, Tonecia Thornton, Raylonda McClinton and the Divas sisterhood, Impact Church Detroit pastor, David John. Aiden, Trinity, and Deon Joy H. Dickerson. To those divinely used on the app "Clubhouse." Lastly, to all those angels I entertained, unaware of those long Uber and Lyft rides to and from work. You all saved my life and made this possible.

Dedication

I would like to dedicate this book to three very important people that I miss dearly. My grandmother. Ronnie Y. Gaddies, who passed away on the cusp of me completing this book. Auntie Carla J. Tillman, I know you would be proud of me. Jimmie A. Lawhorn, I wish you all were here to embrace this accomplishment with me.

-I cannot forget to thank the Struggle for everything and everyone who came up against me, proving that these scars would not overtake me.

-To the reader, thank you for giving my words your attention, and I pray that if you connect with my story in any way, you may be inspired, totally heal, forgive, and love as if you have never been hurt. Know that you, too, can and will be an overcomer.

Brandy Browning

Brandy Browning stands as a cornerstone within the Detroit metropolitan area, revered for her unwavering dedication to families and children as an early childhood development specialist. With a remarkable track record spanning over two decades, she not only owned and managed a profoundly influential development center but also nurtured young minds to achieve their fullest potential both inside and outside the classroom, earning her the status of a true gem in the city.

Even today, families from the past continue to reach out to Mrs. Browning, expressing their gratitude and sharing stories of their children's successes, all testament to the pivotal role she played in their lives. She extends her advocacy beyond her own household, actively serving both families and colleagues alike. Amidst her roles as a devoted wife and mother of three, she carves out time for philanthropic endeavors, organizing events that address critical community needs and collaborating with faith-based organizations to provide clothing and nourishment to those less fortunate, among other initiatives.

Her magnetic personality, a potent blend of power and charisma, effortlessly draws individuals from all generations toward her. With a profound foundation rooted in faith, Brandy possesses a distinctive ability to love unconditionally, irrespective of past hurts, pains, deceptions, or betrayals she may have endured. Aspiring to be an author, a serial entrepreneur, and a steadfast minister, she intends to identify needs and sow seeds of love and kindness wherever her path, guided by God, leads her.

Connect with Brandy
Social media:
Simply B (Brandy Browning) on Facebook
Email: Simplybsimplyb@gmail.com

No Scars Allowed
By Karyn Moss

For some unknown reason, I don't remember much of my childhood. Some are very clear, like my daddy's motorcycle. My dad took me on a ride a few times as a little girl. I remember taking picture next to the motorcycle with my sister. I wore a cute pair of bell-bottom jeans, some Hush puppy brown clogs, and a tan trench coat tied in the front with a pretty bow. My hair was done pretty, and my skin was clear and shiny.

I remember living in Steubenville, Ohio. I lived on Parkview Circle. One of the housing projects there. It was on what we called the hill. I remember my little brother and my older girl cousin. We would play outside. I remember one day riding on my green and yellow Inchworm. I remember my little brother always wanting to ride it; I wouldn't say I liked to share it with him. One day, he got mad at me and pulled me off, and before my older cousin caught me, I hit the ground. I was pissed. I hurt my leg and ran to my mom as I was crying and yelling at him. I always wore dresses when I was younger. My mom came to meet me at the door; I imagine she could hear me crying inside the apartment. I could hear her saying over my yelling, your dad will be so mad. He said, "he does not want you to have scars on your legs." No Scars Allowed is all I could remember her telling me when I was growing up.

I remember moving to Columbus, Ohio, when I was seven years old. We got into a car accident. I got a cut across my nose. I could hear my mom's voice yelling, my baby girl is bleeding. I remember thinking that's going to leave a scar. It did; the scar was visible for most of my adult life. I did not know then that God was a healer. As I said, I always wore dresses when I was younger, and I had to remind myself that my dad said no scars allowed. (After all, I was a tomboy. I had three brothers.) Little did I know I was about to encounter mental, emotional, physical, and spiritual scars.

God is A Protector!

My first mental and emotional scar was when I was about ten. A close person molested me. This was something I did know at the time was not right. It felt wrong, but because I loved this person, I did not realize until years later that it was wrong. I was not even sure that the person knew either. I remember thinking, do all families or someone that loves you do this? I remember always laying down and the person laying on top of me. We'd always have our underwear on. I'm not sure which after a few weeks or months because I was little. I was told to take my underwear off and to I felt something running down my leg. The person yelled at me to run to the tub and take a bath; I remember I had to get in the tub because my house did not have a shower. I remember the person yelling at me to take a bath and wash up so I would not get pregnant. We did not know then, because we were young, that a woman could only get pregnant if she had started her periods.

I screamed at this person to get out of the bathroom, and I threw a fresh bar of soap at the person as they left the bathroom, hitting them in the face. After that day, it never happened again. The pain was still there. I did not know to be embarrassed until years later. I was so ashamed. I had to realize that just because he did not penetrate or we did not have sex, it's not normal for a ten-year-old girl to have that encounter, that physical and emotional experience. I had to say, "Karyn, that is NOT normal, and it's not your fault."

It took me years to know and understand, I had to forgive him. It was not until my late twenties. I had just given my life back to God and knew that forgiveness was for me! I had to forgive myself for being angry at God, and I had to forgive myself for thinking I did something wrong. I never told anyone but my husband what happened to me. I know you are thinking, why? Well, for so long, I did not even think it was wrong. So why would I tell?

A Forgiving God!

I was a teenage mother, I had my oldest son at 15. I was shamed by some church members. His father was the second man I had sex with. I was looking for something I didn't know I needed. I felt like being molested when I was younger was part of how I handled my relationships growing up. I had my second child when I was 19 years old. I love my 3 older children; however, I also wish I could freeze them and have them with my husband I would. I laugh because we know that is not possible. I always blamed GOD for not being there for me but realized I did not invite Him in. I did not allow Him to make the path for me. I choose my path. Thank God for picking me up and setting my feet on the path He needs me to walk. I am grateful for His forgiveness.

God Is A Promise Keeper!

It took me forty years to tell my truth. I blocked this trauma from my mind. I could hear my mom telling me your dad said no scars allowed. I remember thinking my dad was so worried about the scars on my legs. He failed to mention the scars of life and others hurting me. What about telling me how to avoid them? I now know he gave me all that he could, all that he knew how to give. This made me who I am. The trauma and the abuse. My heavenly Father said, no weapon formed against me shall prosper. That is what I stand on to this day. I had to learn to depend and trust my Heavenly Father to give me what I needed.

God IS A HEALER

He healed me! He gave me sight! He delivered me! He forgave me! I tell you, NO SCARS ALLOWED was my thinking for half my life. He brought the DIVAS into my life. God gave me what I always wanted, sisters! One of my best friends, Kenyetta, invited me to listen in.

What an experience! After about the fourth day, I could remember my morning with God reading TD Jake Women Thou Art Loosed bible; the bible has little inscriptions at the bottom of each page. As I was studying, I came across one I had read many times; however, this time, it hit me differently. It read...The more a woman knows that she is accepted and loved by other women who will be honest with her and with whom she can be honest, the less she needs to be handled with kids' gloves.

When she feels it's alright to be herself, she will be less defensive about hiding who she has been or is on the inside. That is what the Divas did for me. I quickly joined. They related to me; better yet, I related to them. These amazing women of God are powerful! They are honest and open—a space to be ourselves. I can accept myself for whom God created me to be, Victorious! I understand I no longer have to be what the world expects me to be. I am no longer a victim! No shame on me; it's shame off me!! I can hear Raylonda telling me. I realized my scars were necessary. They gave me my testimony, my story. As the scars allowed, they gave me what I needed for God to make me strong in Him.

I cried and laughed while writing this chapter. To know that A Diamond is now Revealed because she is ME! Scars No longer cover me.
    I HAVE BEEN DELIVERED, and I AM HEALED!

Acknowledgments

I want to express my love and gratitude to one of my best friends Kenyetta Johnson for being obedient to God and inviting me to the DIVAS. I want to extend my deepest appreciation to my husband, Charles Moss, for support and encouraging me to tell my truths. Thank you for understanding my need to be open and honest. Thank you, readers, for purchasing this book. I pray this book will help you and encourage you with your scars that are still healing. Most of all, I want to give God the honor and praise. Without Him, I am nothing. Thank you, God, for giving me the strength to tell my truths. Thank you for giving me the words to write. Rest in peace, Dad, James West, I love you!

Karyn Moss

Gifted. Healed. Delivered. Victoriously created. Grateful.

You might think that's Karyn's happy ending, but it's really just the beginning! Karyn Moss is a powerhouse woman of God who comes packed with passion for seeking knowledge, understanding, and close personal relationships with women.

The passion she has today for supporting and empowering women definitely came at a price. The same women she's always been drawn to, the ones she always wanted to connect with—were the same ones that rejected, disrespected, and disconnected from her when she was young. Early on, that forced her into a shell, but God's healing enabled her to push through that pain and break out of that shell. Today, she's dedicated her life to serving the very ones who tried to sever her spirit. She simply never gave up on them.

Karyn has made a life of helping, caring, advocating, and serving. She's a 23-year award-winning healthcare communications specialist with a degree in Business Communications. She's currently building the next level of her love walk, Karying 4 God's Kids, a daycare solution for women who are overqualified for government assistance but still struggle to find affordable, quality childcare solutions.

Karyn's your Girl! She is that loyal, dedicated friend who's going to get to know you on a deep, intimate level, the one who really GETS you because she IS you. She's the one who remembers the little things and knows those details that most overlook. She's able to connect with you through her genuine, heartfelt, and humorous approach to relationship-building with her sisters.

Karyn's THAT Girl! She's a fashionista with an eye for interior design and a gift for elevating style. She's the one you want to go shopping with because you know she going to take you to another level! She an anointed Intercessor and anointed for worshiping the Lord through dance. This Dancing Queen is highly acclaimed for her gift as she serves in her church dance ministry.

As a wife, mother of 4, and Ya Ya to 13, Karyn's triumphant tale of love and impact is still being written daily. Get ready to see a bit of yourself in this excerpt of her journey to victory.

Karyn can be reached at:
karynmoss2019@gmail.com

I Thought I Was Healed
By Kenyatta Johnson

Naturally, we have questions, right? Why is it so hard to obey what God tells us to do? It comes down to becoming obedient and then surrendering our will for the WILL OF GOD. This is why I said God is a gentleman. He lets us choose what we want to do with our life. Well, I know what you're probably disagreeing about, but think about it: Are you forced to do things you don't want to do? Life is serious; our lives are based upon our decisions and choices and the direction we want to take.

Okay, okay, okay, I'm hearing opposition. I know what you're thinking, that it's out of our control, and we had to make choices and decisions based on that standpoint. I'm speaking of the choice we made that wasn't forced. Now, I have a story; do you want to hear it? Here we go...

Psst, come here; I want to share something. Is that okay? I want you to be aware that I am here this time to give insight and understanding into the journey you are about to embark upon. You know God is a gentleman. He is never going to force His will upon you. Yeah, right, I'm being serious. He is the most gentle and loving person you will ever meet. I found this out in a very hard way. He is like a loving parent who will allow you to do things your way until you become sick of yourself and surrender to His will. He will allow you to try the situation, circumstance, or scenario you plan, and then it's like he has a sense of humor. He asks you, Abigail, How's that plan working out for you? Don't mind me. I call Him a comedian from time to time because I am like you, seriously!!! Are you going to do me like this? I'm not laughing.

He wants permission to enter your heart and be included in our daily lives and situations. He's not going to overstep his boundaries, but he will send you clues in different ways along your journey to help you see things clearly. You can ask him right now to come into your heart and situation and he will do just that. By saying, I thank you for allowing this moment, I confess with my mouth and believe in my heart that Jesus died for my sins and I believe you rose on the third day, and one day you are coming back for me. Lord, come into my heart and forgive me of my sins and wash and cleanse me, Lord, come into my situation, and I permit you to guide me in the right direction. I give my life to you. Lord, I need you to help me get back on track. Thank you for never leaving me alone, and I'm trusting you. In Jesus' name, Amen. Lord, we seal this prayer with the blood of Jesus and ask that you send your angels of protection and guide them in the way they should go. Congratulations, Jesus loves you, and so do I.

Psst, it's me again. I'm back with another story since this is a safe place. I want to share my heart with you; I know you're like, what do you mean again? Put it like this: the last time I felt like this, I made a series of wrong choices, and my life was turned upside down.

This time, I feel it is happening again, but even though my flesh is screaming, I'm choosing to walk in obedience. The pain is significant and costly, but I want to walk in obedience to God because he has allowed me to see myself and loves me with all my flaws and messes. He has never turned his back on me. Yet He walked me out of a terrible situation and provided a way of escape. He gave me a space to express my discontent with my situation without judgment and, in the most loving way, allowed me to vent and express my anger. I blamed other people, and I said all the bad things about things happening, and God wrapped his loving arms around me and held me close as if to say, Do you need a hug, daughter? In those moments, I would sob, weep, cry, and find out that if no one else loves me, GOD LOVES ME.

Now it is time to walk in obedience, having faith and trusting God to get me through my discomfort and this dis- ease I feel, knowing God wants better for me. Obedience is indeed a choice of the heart. Where is your heart position at this time? I know you have said or heard this before: follow your heart. I was once in agreement with that until, until what? Disaster turned my life upside down, and I crashed and burned; I followed my heart. My heart was sick and full of pride. The sacrifice had become greater. Greater because I don't have the time to repeat and try to fix things and make corrections. Walking in obedience might be painful, but the outcome is that I won't have to go backward to come forward again. I want more than enough. I want to walk in obedience and live free. For once, I can say, without any doubt, that it was better to listen to the voice of God inside of me. I've come to realize that God wants us to follow him with our whole hearts. His word declares. Jesus said unto him, Thou shalt love the Lord thy God with all thy heart, and with all thy soul, and with all thy mind. (Matthew 22:37 KJV)

This is not to say that following God will be easy or a cakewalk. By no means do I want to mislead you in any way. I believe walking in obedience to God will require something from us.

We must be doers of God's word, be humble, submit to God, and love God more than anything or anyone. It's one thing to say you're going to do something or want to do things to become better in your walk with God, but can I tell you today that's all hogwash!!! I said it to say, what will you do without any follow through? Why am I saying this? You have to put action behind your purpose when coming to God.

Be a doer in this season.

Don't just sit idle in your situation and expect it will miraculously happen. You must move; you must do what he has asked (James 1: 22- 25). KJV says, be ye doers of the word and not hearers only deceiving yourself.

So, in other words, when we don't put action behind God's word and do what his word tells us to do, we leave an open place for deception to creep in because of what he said but don't do anything about it or if you do the total opposite. As long as we say things and do nothing about it, it's like blowing hot air; it escapes and evaporates. No one can trust what you say because no action supports your words. You merely talking isn't making me believe the words that come out of your mouth until you put some effort behind them. (And Let the Church Say Amen____amen)

We must be humble.

It was defined as not proud or haughty, not arrogant, assertive, reflecting, expressing, or offering in a spirit of defense or submission. I know you probably need a Selah after that message, so pause. Breathe. Exhale. Breathe. Exhale.

Now, are you still with me? I know that was a lot in a short time. As I told you today, Jesus and I love you.

Let's continue. Get comfortable, and let's have a chat, a chat about what?

I'm glad you asked. Let's talk about humility. It's the way of taking the high road when someone thinks they have won. Have you ever been in a situation that called for you to become humble even when you felt you had the right to take another person down? Be slow to speak. Instead, you said, you're right; it's like giving someone a pass or some grace. I consider myself humble, although a few people would say otherwise. LOL, I've heard the phrase got to have the last word; I say well, I have one more thing to say.

I remember like yesterday when God told me I could no longer respond to what was happening around me. The words "be still, just watch." In my mind, I felt I was being abused mentally. One of the worst things for me then was being unable to say anything to the person or people who had wronged me. Oh Lord, don't you hear what they are saying? That's not true. Lord, see how they are treating me as if we just met. Lord, can I just... Handle it? His answer was... No, say nothing!!!

I had to sit among the very people inflicting pain upon me. I had to endure the laughing in my face, I had to endure the gossip, I had to endure. At the same time, I was being ignored, I had to cry myself through the pain, and I had to watch others continue to live happily as I sat in silence and suffering. I wanted to lash out; I wanted to scream; I tried to smash people and tell them where they could go. I wanted to treat them as they did me.

Instead, God said the Egyptians you see today, you will see no more, (Exodus 14: 13). If you're anything like me, I wanted people to know that I had been done wrong, and I wanted to tell people about the truth of the matter, but God said NO. Don't say anything! You have heard this spoken before a soft answer turns away wrath. Sometimes, silence in a heavy situation can speak volumes. In the moment of silence, the Lord's voice becomes the loudest. When you enter your secret place, you will begin to hear what thus saith the Lord.

The Lord gives you strength when you are humble. Obedience will require you to become humble in this hour. When we are at our weakest moment, allow God's strength to be perfect in our weakness. In those moments, the Lord will delight Himself in you and crown you with victory.

We must submit.

For a long time, I misunderstood the true meaning of submit. We all have these made-up definitions of the word until we look it up. Submissive means ready to conform to the authority or will of others.

Psst.. Are you there? Are you still there? I hope so; I don't want to leave you behind. I want to continue our conversation to ensure we walk this obedient thing to the finish line. It's not easy to stay obedient to the will of God, but I can say that God is ever so true to his word. If we submit ourselves to God and resist the devil, he will flee (James 4:7).

We must remember that for God to move, it will also require us to do our part. We cannot just sit idly by and expect God to move mountains. You can attest to God having some requirements. Submit and apply resistance for the enemy to flee. There is a level that we are expected to meet, if you will. The requirement doesn't seem complicated when written on paper, but when you start putting into action the words you have now read, you will find movement. There is going to be a shift. The word of God is life. The Word was God, and the Word was life according to (John 1:4). In him was life, and life was like of men.

So because the end of God is life, it has movement. Read the word, remember to put action behind what you read, and be a doer of his word and not just a hearer. We have to make his word **active** in our lives. We have to activate our minds to receive the word, and store it in our hearts so that we do not sin against him. So, activation comes by hearing when we have faith to hear what God has told us to do, then use our faith to put the word we have read into action and do what he has said. Most of what we know in our head needs action so we can now obey God's word. Walking in obedience brings for Honor.

For instance, have you ever felt your spirit become uneasy when God wants you to change? There have been moments where I could tell something in my spirit was happening, my mood would change, and I would become emotional in certain situations. I would notice something was feeling different, or people would act funny. Better yet, I heard God speak to me through someone else's testimony. Someone will speak to my situation or confirm something in my spirit. This is when I knew God had shifted my atmosphere, and let me say this: sometimes you may not be ready, but God is ready for you.

Alright then.

What he is trying to get us to understand is that he is not going to be put on PAUSE any longer.

Time out for, " Lord, wait,"
Time over for" I'm not ready," "I'm waiting for the right time," and Time out for, "Lord, did you say?"
Yeah, He said it!
Yeah, He chose you!
Yeah, He needs you!
Yeah, He got you!
Now, pick up your bed and walk into obedience!!!

Sometimes, we got all the excuses about why something won't work and what someone else will think or say. Most of the time, we need to get out of our heads. Allow God to use you and be obedient. Please, ma'am, please, sir! Have you ever felt God was silent or stopped speaking to you? Let me tell you this: I was sitting in my room listening to worship music, praying, and asking God what I should do now. Well, my answer didn't come on the day on which I prayed; I was in the middle of a conversation with someone and God spoke clearly and said write the book. I'm thinking to myself, I never considered myself to be a writer. Besides, what do I have to write about? God said, your story.

During this time in my life so much was happening to me; it seemed all at once. I was uprooted out of a familiar place, placed in a new state and changed my friendships and comfortable places.

When God began to move in such a way, you recognized his love. These are those he loved to sing with me; he loves us, and Oh How He Loves Us.

God loves us so much that if we go left, he will send a rod of correction to get us back on the path he desires us to be. He sends a gentle guide along the way. His tender mercies and loving-kindness are new every morning. He sends his messenger angels to protect us when we stumble and fall, and he covers us under the shadow of his wings.

He loves us so much that while we were sinners, Christ died for us. He has shown us his love for us from the very beginning.

There is something that I found out about God. It didn't matter how frustrated I was; he still loved me. It didn't matter how much anger I had built inside me. He still loved me. It didn't matter that I was screaming and yelling at him because I was angry and in pain. He still loves me. It didn't matter to him that I was cussing and wanting revenge; he still loved me.

What matters to him is that I turn to him in my time of need. I repented and cried out to him, the only one who could pull me up out of the darkness. He is there with open arms, saying come to me as you are. Just as the prodigal son was greeted with open arms, so is Our God standing in front of you with his arms ready to receive you, my dear child. In moments like this, we should cast our cares upon the Lord, who cares or us. In the arms of God is where I have regained my sanity. In the arms of God that I found my refuge and my peace. It is in the arms of God that he gave me his strength so I could make it another day. It is in the arms of God that I found him to be my protection. It's in the arms of God that I was my most vulnerable, and God loved me through the process.

Just understand this...

No matter what is going on, God is in the midst. He heard my cry, and He sent me peace. I want to let you know that he can handle all human frustration and get us all together. God will chasten those he loves. This love and allowed me to take His yoke upon me, for His yoke is easy and His burdens are light. He has forgiven me; His love is unconditional; He has restored me; He has sustained me. Oh, how I love Jesus because He first loved me.

Dedication

First, I give honor and all praise to my God, who has led me and guided me throughout my journey called life. Without him, none of this would have been possible.

I want to dedicate my chapter to my mom, who is undoubtedly my biggest cheerleader and one of the few who even knew this was happening. I thank you for always believing in me and encouraging me. When I saw you at your lowest, I watched God bring you through it. I watched how you held on to God and fought and persevered through pain and any obstacle put in your way. I praise God for you, Mommy. I see you, and I love you!

To my children, who are the absolute joys of my life. I am a mother because God saw it fit to bless my life with two amazing children. I kept going when times were hard because I had you two to fight for. Although you guys are grown and living life, I can only be excited about your future and know I have done my best to raise you to the best of my ability.

I dedicate this chapter to both of you, my future, in hopes that you continue to prosper in the Lord, knowing that all things are possible with God. Just trust God and allow your light to shine wherever you go.

To my grandchild, who means so much to me. I can't explain how all my emotions flooded me when I saw you enter this world. You are such a light and a special part of Nana's life. I love how you share your learning adventures in school, love God, and sing his praises. I pray this will inspire you one day to go further than me.

To my brothers, I love you guys so much. Thank you for always being there for me. Thank you for having my back.

To my family and friends, I dedicate this to you in hopes that you know that it is never too late to move forward and do what God has told you to do. As long as you are still here on earth, you have time to complete the assignment God has placed on your life. Go forth in Jesus' Name.

Acknowledgments

I am a part of a Sisterhood called DIVAS. It is truly an amazing turn of events that brought us together. Without God's connection, this would not be possible. Being a part of this book wouldn't have happened if this amazing woman of God had not opened the door to too many, and I decided to take a leap of faith and become a part of this life-changing moment. I am truly grateful for Raylonda McClinton coming into my life, speaking life back into me, praying for me, and encouraging me when I had no idea what I was doing. You saw the gifts. You have allowed me to grow and created a safe place to land where women from all walks of life can be themselves without fear or judgment. Thank you for this amazing opportunity, and thank you for your obedience to God. Thank you to my Clubhouse DIVAS, who prayed for me through one of the most challenging, humbling experiences. We have cried together, laughed, and celebrated with one another. I am truly grateful for you being in my life. Thank you for allowing God to help push me when I was ready to give up, when it got hard, and walk away when things got rough, but God used you to call me, and check up on me. I have many to thank, and when you start calling names, I might forget someone, which is never intentional.

To my church family, ALL Saints Temple COGIC, Pastor Wilbur Allen III.

Kenyatta Johnson

Kenyatta Johnson is an Ohio native who has a fun, energetic, spontaneous, and joyful personality and is passionate about serving the community in a variety of ways. Whether it is through volunteer work at her local church, working during Vacation Bible School, food bank, or always being available when called upon to use her gifts of ministering through prayer or song. She has allowed her talents and gifts to make room for her in her life. She continues to labor as a faithful intercessor, teacher, and administrator. It has truly been a labor of love serving as a current leader within DIVAS, a non-profit organization whose sole purpose is to educate, empower, equip, and encourage women from all walks of life.

In the professional arena, Kenyatta has worked in Early Childhood Education for 14 years, helping to rear the young minds of the future by giving them the necessary tools they would need to navigate through life by encouraging them to learn new social and emotional skills and preparing them for a new direction when they graduate to kindergarten.

Kenyatta is a devoted mother of two awesome children and Nana to one amazing granddaughter, a daughter, a sister, an auntie, and a cousin to many.

Kenyatta can be reached outside this platform:
www.instagram.com/kenyaattajohnson
Facebook: KenyattaJohnson
Email: IthoughtIwashealed@gmail.com

Clawing Out Of The Muddy Pit
By Niambi Carriere

He brought me up out of a horrible pit, out of the miry clay, set my feet upon a rock, and established my goings. And he hath put a new song in my mouth, even praise unto our God: many shall see it, fear, and trust in the Lord.
Psalms 40:2-4 King James Version

Leaving the Hospital

I thought that no one should ever leave the hospital without their child. I felt like I had fallen into a muddy pit. Pure silence, numbness, shock, and disbelief accompanied me as I and my family walked out those doors the morning of May 28, 2020. My 12-year-old son, Uriah, had succumbed to asthma complications. How could he be here one day and gone the next? Hours prior, his life on earth was winding down. I slowly turned and stared past the clear glass as the orange and yellow sun rays stretched over the horizon. All I could think of was how beautiful it was and how extraordinary peace washed over me. God had painted every brushstroke to comfort me in the moment. I was so thankful that I could witness His presence in the midst of an escalating pandemic and my son's unexpected death.

I was on autopilot and had no recollection of how I got to our SUV or even home. I unlocked the door to a quiet house as if we were empty nesters. Within twenty-four hours, our atmosphere had drastically shifted from the noise level of three kids to a family that had felt lost without one. Our words were few as I scanned the room in reflection; earlier in the week, Uriah had finished his schoolwork ahead of time for his sixth-grade year. His intense focus was on the TV, with his thumbs rapidly tapping the game controller. He grazed on snacks and binge-watched movies he hadn't seen before. Extended periods of screen time weren't the norm, but virtual school for him was complete. I remember he had expressed wanting to be homeschooled at one time or another earlier in the school year. God knew his heart's desire and granted it.

Getting the Word Out

The next day, reality didn't feel real. Our extended family knew. I dreaded the tasks, and I could no longer put them off. My cell phone felt like a brick. Uriah's best friend needed to know. I choked back the tears to relay to my friend, Uriah's best friend's mom, and that Uriah had died. It wasn't an easy conversation.

As I hung up the phone, I sat before my large-screened computer. My fingertips and thoughts were out of sync. How would I tell everyone that he was gone? I hesitated and slowly tried to assemble the right words on the screen as tears trickled down my face. My fingers pressed the keys with inconsistent pauses. Just breath. String together another sentence one by one. I mustered up the energy and strength to compile emails to my kids' principals and highlight the teachers who had poured into Uriah and the girls over the years. Then, I pressed send.

After the emails had gone out, the support poured in. My adrenaline kicked in. Burial arrangements were at the top of the list. Due to the severity of the escalating pandemic, a traditional funeral and burial fell by the wayside. No wake. No funeral. No family and friends gathered in a church or at the graveside—only phone conversations and texts. Our simplistic plans were now for a family of four with an empty seat at the table. We grieved quietly in isolation without our animated middle child. However, this time felt like a gift. Our emotions were raw. We had a padlock and a "do not enter sign" for protection. The isolation gave us time to grieve without restrictions, opinions, and misunderstandings.

Surprise in the Mailbox

Days later, I walked to the mailbox. I reached in, and one particular envelope stood out. "To the parents of Uriah Carriere, it read." It was from the school district. I knew exactly what it was...his grades. I briefly paused and delicately opened the envelope. Tears welled in my eyes as I unfolded his report card as all "A's" for the school year jumped off the page. All of his hard work had paid off. He finished strong despite his busy schedule of being Student Council President, an orchestra member, and the Boys to Gentlemen organization, along with his accomplishments. With a smile, I quietly said, "You did it, baby. You made all A's for the year, and I'm so proud of you".

Summertime

The summer was a blur and hijacked of the usual laughter, summer camp, and fun. I was engulfed in medical bills and inching my way through tasks since our world had roadblocks from the pandemic. I inquired about counseling but briefly tabled it, unsure what I needed.

New School Year

The new school year, August 2020, crept up on us, and my emotions were entangled like a big ball of string. A lack of preparedness plagued me physically, mentally, and emotionally. I tried to be ready, but it was as if my fingernails only passed through the sludge that my hands could not hold. We started the school year without Uriah. It was unfathomable to believe there was one less to buy for, one less school dropoff, and one less hug. Uriah's absence equated to an illusion, which left a void in our family. However, God reminded me that He would never leave or forsake us, even when walking through hard things.

Searching for Support

In August 2020, I picked back up searching for support. Resources were available, but it felt like looking for a lost bracelet on a beach. It made my head spin. Then, I had a flashback of the hospital social worker with papers recommending a place for a grief group. My fingers flipped through the pages, and I found it. "Ok, "I'll start with this one." It was great and served my needs. However, I started surfing the internet, and another resource popped up. After pushing send on the inquiry for more information and a phone call or two, I found another group that I thought would be helpful. It had a smaller setting and gave more time to process the grief. Unbeknownst to me, it led to one-on-one therapy, a deeper dive.

Health Crisis

In August of 2021, while dealing with the grief of my son, I was still helping my dad, who had a heart attack in 2019. My energy level had tanked to add another layer to grief, and slow motion became the norm. I couldn't put my finger on it. The bloodwork revealed the underlying issues. I was diagnosed with diabetes and anemia.

Appointment after appointment and test after test, I was able to have a clearer picture of where I was physically. With a lot of prayer, the doctor's care, medication, supplements, and nutrition, I was starting to climb out of exhaustion. My numbers started changing, and my bloodwork confirmed that my health was improving.

New Church and DIVAS

In the summer of 2022, a friend persistently extended invitations to her church. As a caterpillar transforms into a butterfly, with God's help and our new church, many witnessed the deliverance and healing that would transpire over the next year.

Around this time, I joined a new audio app called Clubhouse. I surfed through different rooms and worked on learning the platform. One day, I stumbled across the DIVAS room. I had no idea of what I had stumbled across. Sisters from Detroit, MI, and around the country would change my life forever. I remember hearing Raylonda's voice, our visionary, and I kept thinking she sounded like my cousin. Her voice exuded authority and power, lined with sweetness, and her unforgettable laugh was infectious. My broken heart had endured so much, and these ladies welcomed me immediately. As I allowed the process of peeling back the layers of hurt and pain, I realized that I was becoming whole. I knew this sisterhood could be impactful, and I had found my new tribe.

Healing Journey

Since 2020 and beyond, I will continue on my healing journey. I ensured I had spiritual, mental, emotional, relationally, financial, and physical support to maintain my healing. My tribe of people God put in my life (family, friends, various ministries, the school district, the church, mentors, and DIVAS, etc.). There's no way I could have done this on my own. The Lord's help and guidance brought me through one of the most challenging seasons of my life. If you are wondering if you can survive hard stuff, such as the death of a loved one, you can! It is possible. Keep moving forward!

The season shaped me, molded me, and refined me. It taught me to lean on the Lord and never give up. He helped me to claw my way out of that muddy pit. I belly crawled until I could rise and stand again. His word, the Bible, steadied me so I could walk again. Others came alongside me, and I pushed myself to run again. I stretched myself to laugh again. I trusted our Lord and Savior, and He healed me. No longer bound, covered by scars, and refined by the process. Now, I'm a diamond revealed to display God's heart healing, and you can experience it, too!

Strength and honor are her clothing; and she shall rejoice in time to come.
Proverbs 31:25 King James Version

Takeaways

So many people and resources contributed to my healing journey, and it's impossible to document everything. Since everyone's situation is different, this may or may not apply to you. However, I will do my best to share some of the major contributors that helped me to get on the other side of grief, and there may be organizations in your local area that provide similar resources and services.

These are just a few actions that have made a huge difference in my journey:

- My relationship with the Lord - not staying stuck in the muddy pit
- The Bible
- My prayer life
- Consistency in going to church and bible study
- Prayers of positive influencers (family, friends, and mentors)
- Support (spiritual, physical, mental, emotional, and financial) for me and my family
- Wise counsel
- Music (gospel, Christian, soaking music, and inspirational)
- Anointing Routines (my home and myself)
- Journaling

These are some of the resources I utilized:

- Bo's Place - https://www.bosplace.org/en/
- Flourish Now - https://www.flourishnowlive.com/
- Grief Recovery Group - https://www.griefrecoverymethod.com/
- Hope Again Counseling - https://www.hopeagaincounseling.com/
- Joan Hunter Ministries - https://joanhunter.org/
- Journey U - https://www.journeyu.org/
- DIVAS - https://divas8.wildapricot.org/

Declarations

I declare and decree:

- Grief doesn't own me.
- It's okay for me to feel, grieve, and go through this process.
- Grief has no timeline, and I am free to make the choices that work for me in this season of my life.
- I will get through this.
- I am victorious.
- I will live a fulfilling life with joy.
- I will walk in the fruit of the spirit.
- My joy will return.
- My peace will return.
- My future will be bright. I will always love my loved ones and will miss them.
- I will cherish my memories of loved ones with a smile and not grief must go! What goes in your blank? For me, trauma, grief, pain, trigger points, fear, anxiety, etc.
- I am whole.
- No scar is too deep that can't be healed by God.
- Joy and healing await me on the other side of grief, pain, and suffering.
- I will live a life of no regrets.

Strength and honor are her clothing; and she shall rejoice in time to come.
Proverbs 31:25 King James Version

End Notes:

2 Corinthians 5:8 King James Version
Psalms 40:2-4 King James Version
Proverbs 31:25 King James Version

Dedication

This chapter is dedicated to Uriah Seth Carriere (September 14, 2007 - May 28, 2020). He was the middle child, intelligent, observant, animated, and funny, the peacemaker, an intuitive and humble old soul of many talents (musician, dancer, athlete, communicator, and a leader) with an infectious laugh. We love you, miss you, and honor your legacy! We will see you again!

I say we are confident and willing rather than be absent from the body and present with the Lord.
2 Corinthians 5:8 King James Version.

Acknowledgments

I want to say thank you to so many. Multiple people and organizations played a huge role in me and my family's lives, even some I didn't know personally. The amount of space on this page is insufficient to list every name. I appreciate everyone who contributed to helping us walk out this journey. Thank you to The Carriere family, my parents, Richard Laws, Juanita Gaines, and Willis Gaines, Sr., The Laws Family, The Breaux Family, The Luckie Family, The Speech family, The Berrios Family, The Tomball ISD family, Church families (Freedom House, Church 1:37, Champion Forest Baptist Church, Church of Champions, and Intimidad Con Dios), many friends, classmates, you know who you are and stepped up to help (too many to count), Flourish Now, Dayna Belcher, Kathy Heiliger, Joan Hunter Ministries, Bo's Place, Hope Again Counseling, Grief Recovery Method, Laura Bradshaw, Journey U and team, Uriah's classmates and families, our neighbors, Global and Company Real Estate, Barajas Enterprises, and last but not least, The DIVAS organization along with visionary of DIVAS, Raylonda McClinton.

Niambi Carriere

Niambi is a passionate educator, a detail-oriented virtual assistant, and a caregiver emergency preparedness enthusiast. Niambi is best known as a passionate educator who has served in multiple capacities inside and out outside of the school setting as a lifelong learner. Recently, Niambi transitioned into a new role as a virtual assistant within the estate planning and retirement planning industries, which has allowed her to expand her career at a critical time in history. This role has confirmed and spotlighted the necessity of caregivers of aging parents and their children to have essential documentation ready.

When tragedy struck her home with the sudden death of her 12-year-old son, Uriah, in May of 2020, she had a choice. Would she stay stuck in grief or rise above the circumstances and push forward? Pushing forward catapulted her to a new level. She advocates for other moms whose child(ren) has died and embraces being a beacon of hope for healing and freedom that awaits them on the other side of grief and loss. Niambi's strategies have allowed her to walk out on her journey with more joy, wisdom, and freedom than before due to her faith in Christ.

Email: niambi@niambicarriere.com
FB: https://www.facebook.com/niambi.laws.carriere
LinkedIn: https://www.linkedin.com/in/niambi-l-carriere
Instagram: https://www.instagram.com/niambicarriere/

Made in the USA
Columbia, SC
12 December 2023